No matter what always is: How to do

The mind has m more than you have ev ....ned of—and human-ity has barely begun the wonderful evolutionary journey that will let us tap into them all at will. We grow in our abilities as we do things.

There are many wonderful things you can do. As you do them, you learn more about the innate qualities of mind and spirit, and as you exercise these inner abilities, they will grow in strength—*as will your vision of your mental and spiritual potential.*

In learning to *Uncover Your Past Lives,* or See and Read the Aura, or making a Love Charm, or using a Magic Mirror , or many other strange and wonderful things, you are extending—just a little bit—the tremendous gift that lies within, the Life Force itself.

We are born that we may grow, and not to use this gift—not to grow in your perception and understanding of it—is to turn away from the gifts of Life, of Love, of Beauty, of Happiness that are the very reason for Creation.

Learning how to do these things is to open psychic windows to New Worlds of Mind & Spirit. Actually doing these things is to enter into New Worlds. Each of these things that we do is a step forward in accepting responsibility for the worlds that you can shape and influence.

Simple, easy to follow, yet so very rewarding. Following these step-by-step instructions can start you upon high adventure. Gain control over the world around you, and step into *New Worlds of Mind & Spirit.*

About the Author

Ted Andrews is a full time author, student and teacher in the metaphysical and spiritual fields. He conducts seminars, symposiums, and workshops and lectures throughout the country on many facets of ancient mysticism. Ted works with past life analysis, aura interpretation, numerology, the tarot and the qabala as methods of developing and enhancing inner potential. He is a clairvoyant and a certified spiritualist medium. Ted is also active in the healing field. He is certified in basic hypnosis and acupressure and is involved in the study and use of herbs.

To Write to the Author

We cannot guarantee that every letter written to the author can be answered, but all will be forwarded. Both the author and the publisher appreciate hearing from readers, learning of your enjoyment and benefit from this book. Llewellyn also publishes a bimonthly news magazine with news and reviews of practical esoteric studies and articles helpful to the student, and some readers' questions and comments to the author may be answered through this magazine's columns if permission to do so is included in the original letter. The author sometimes participates in seminars and workshops, and dates and places are announced in The Llewellyn New Times. To write to the author, or to ask a question, write to:

Ted Andrews
c/o The Llewellyn New Times
P.O. Box 64383-022, St. Paul, MN
Please enclose a self-addressed, stamped envelope for reply, or
$1.00 to cover costs.

Llewellyn's How To Series

How To Uncover Your Past Lives

Ted Andrews

1992
Llewellyn Publications
P.O. Box 64383, St. Paul, MN 55164-0383, U.S.A.

FIRST EDITION

Cover painting by Martin Cannon

Library of Congress Cataloging in Publication Data
Andrews, Ted, 1952-
    How to uncover your past lives / Ted Andrews.
        p. cm.—(Llewellyn's how to series)
    Includes bibliographical references.
    ISBN 0-87542-022-2 : $3.95
    1. New Age movement.   2. Reincarnation.
        3. Hypnotism.   4. Karma.   5. Transcendental
        meditation.   I. Title.   II. Series.
    BP605.N48A53   1991
    133.9'01'3—dc20
                                           91 44586
                                           CIP

Llewellyn Publications
A Division of Llewellyn Worldwide, Ltd.
P.O. Box 64383, St. Paul, MN 55164-0383

Dedication

For my family, friends and students—
particularly my special Columbus family
for their support, friendship and
loving humor!

"Vocatus atque non vocatus, Deus aderat."

Other Books by Ted Andrews

Forthcoming:

Other Books in Llewellyn's How To Series

CONTENTS

1

Understanding Reincarnation

We may never be able to prove that we have lived before. Even if we are able to produce names, dates and places, it still does not prove that we lived at that time and place. So why write a book on uncovering past lives? Because, even without conclusive proof, the benefits for personal empowerment, healing and enlightenment are tremendous.

Reincarnation means different things to different people. It is a theory, a philosophy, a belief system and a way of life. It explains many of the unexplained occurrences of life. It provides a rationale for the inequalities and the suffering of life. It gives us insight into our many individual differences.

More importantly, reincarnation provides a model for behavior and living based on personal responsibility. This book will help show that you are the master of your own destiny. It will teach you that what you are today is the result of your past and that what you will become tomorrow is determined by how you live today.

To many this can be very frightening. It eliminates those devils, demons and other scapegoats for the conditions of our lives. At the same time it is very exciting, for it helps us to realize that we truly can write the scripts of our lives.

This book will help you explore your past lives and realize that they have helped shape and mold you into who you are right now. You will begin to see that you are a synthesis of all that has gone before. As this realization increases through the uncovering of your past lives, your ability to control and reshape your life will also increase. You will become more active within all of life's processes. Instead of sitting back and allowing events to simply play upon you, you will be able to see them from a new and proper perspective and thus act accordingly. No longer will you have to bang your head against the wall and cry: "Why is this always happening to me? Why do I always run into these same kinds of people and situations?" This book will help you see the larger patterns of life within your own individual circumstances.

Literally, reincarnation means the return to the physical body. It is the belief that the soul, upon death, exits one body and begins to prepare to come back into life within another physical form. The circumstances of that return—the environment and such—are determined by the growth and progress achieved in the previous lives. Each life personality is a synthesis of what has gone before, and its rebirth occurs in an environment that can best unfold and build upon it for its greater benefit. Thus, the better we live our lives, the more beneficial our rebirth circumstances will be.

Some areas of the world have taught that the soul could come back as anything within the physical—from a tree to an insect to another human being, but often as an animal. One such example comes through the African Zulu tradition, as is reported by Sylvia Cranston and Carey Williams in their book *Reincarnation—A New Horizon in Science, Religion and Society* (Julian Press; New York, 1984; pages 164-166):

> Within the body is a soul: within the soul is a spark of Itango, the universal spirit. After the death of the body, Idhozi (the soul) hovers for a while near the body and then departs to Esilweni, the Place of the Beasts. In Esilweni the soul assumes a shape part beast, part human, before it rises higher.... According to the strength of the animal nature, the soul throws aside its beast like shape and moves onward to a place of rest. There it sleeps, till a time comes when it dreams that something to do and learn awaits it on earth; then it awakes and returns to earth and is born again as a child. The soul repeats this until it becomes one with the Itongo (the universal spirit).

This assuming of a shape part beast is different from entering the body of a beast, and it actually is similar to eastern teachings of the *bardo* and even some teachings of purgatory, where the animal nature must be thrown off before the purified soul can ascend to heaven. Seers have claimed to have seen newly departed humans wearing the garment of animals that corresponds to their earthly nature. This could have been misconstrued into a belief that humans incarnate into animals.

This book will approach the theory of reincarnation only from the human level; i.e., the soul clothing itself in another human body. What will be provided is merely a skeletal framework. It will enable you to begin your own exploration process. It is not within the scope of this work to explore the full philosophic and theoretical implications of the reincarnation process.

An incarnation is a period of existence within the body. It is only half of a developmental cycle. The full developmental cycle is the time from one birth into the physical until the next rebirth. From the moment of conception until the physical transition we call death is half of this period. It is sometimes called the mundane or physical phase. The second half is that period from the moment of death till the moment of rebirth. It is sometimes called the cosmic or spiritual interim.

The mundane phase begins at the moment of conception. At this moment the consciousness of the incoming soul begins to align itself with the fertilized egg. Because the true soul energy is so dynamic and intense, it cannot fully integrate with the developing vehicle immediately. It uses that nine month period of pregnancy to slow its vibrational intensity down so that, at or around the time of birth, it can integrate fully and safely with the fetus. The consciousness of the soul is aligned with increasing intensity throughout the entire pregnancy. (This mystery and that of the death transition, along with their roles in the evolution of the soul, will be explored more fully in chapter 5.)

The cosmic or spiritual interim begins at the moment of the transition called death. One of the most common questions asked is what happens during that interim period between incarnations. This period enables the soul to recuperate, reassess and assimilate the experiences of the previous life, along with preparing for the next. We must keep in mind that our greatest and most intense learning comes through our physical life experiences. These experiences, great and small, must be assimilated and placed within proper perspective.

The interim enables the soul to refresh itself after the intensity of the physical life. It enables the soul and those physical life experiences to be illumined by Divine Mind. It serves to strengthen the faculties of the soul and to prepare the soul to return to earth and work out any compensations still needed, while encountering new learnings to

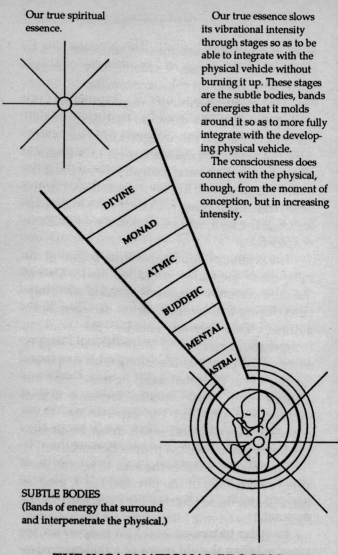

Our true spiritual essence.

Our true essence slows its vibrational intensity through stages so as to be able to integrate with the physical vehicle without burning it up. These stages are the subtle bodies, bands of energies that it molds around it so as to more fully integrate with the developing physical vehicle.

The consciousness does connect with the physical, though, from the moment of conception, but in increasing intensity.

DIVINE

MONAD

ATMIC

BUDDHIC

MENTAL

ASTRAL

SUBTLE BODIES
(Bands of energy that surround
and interpenetrate the physical.)

THE INCARNATIONAL PROCESS

add to its overall growth. The preparations for the ideal time, place and conditions for this to occur take time.

This separation of one developmental cycle can be easily symbolized by the ancient Eastern Yin and Yang symbol (see next page). The dark area is symbolic of our time within the physical, and the light area is the time outside of the physical body. The white circle within the dark area is the soul inherent within the physical life. The black circle within the light area is the physical life circumstances which add to our spiritual and soul growth, which we assimilate during the spiritual interim. The wavy line that separates the two phases can symbolize the continual movement of life adding to life, spiritual to the physical and physical to the spiritual.

Although this is not the traditional interpretation for this symbol, it is one that I have found effective in meditation upon the life, death and rebirth processes. It helps awaken a greater sense of infinity and connectedness within our own individual life circumstances. It keeps alive the realization that we cannot separate the spiritual from the physical, birth from death or death from rebirth. It can open the door to understanding cycles within your own development.

In order to understand how it operates, we must redefine the old terms of fatalism, predestination and heredity.

A SYMBOL OF REINCARNATION

In this ancient Eastern symbol, we can see the mysteries of reincarnation. The black side is that half of the developmental cycle we spend in the physical, and the white side is the half we spend within the spiritual. Together they make one cycle of growth. Because it is a circle, though, it never ends. One cycle always becomes another. Our growing and unfolding never ends.

Fatalism is the belief that we are born into a materialistic world and that our place within that world is simply due to some kind of lottery. We have come from nowhere—by no real law of justice, love or forgiveness—and when we die we pass on into nothingness again. For anyone who believes in a beneficent divine force within the universe, this concept just will not work. Why strain, study and try to do well in life if it is all for nothing? It's a terribly depressing view of life.

Predestination is the belief that, by some divine decree of God or the divine forces of the universe, some humans and angels are predestined to success and everlasting life while others are ordained to everlasting death. Again this is a terribly pessimistic view of life. And what truly divine force would act in such a human and arbitrary fashion?

This view of predestination will be altered somewhat when we look at the laws of karma and compensation at play within the reincarnation process in chapter 2. What we hope to show within this book is that how we live our lives now sets the tone for what we will experience in the future. We predestine ourselves—for good, bad or indifferent. We cannot blame it on some distant divine force. We write the scripts, and we play the parts of the scripts we have written.

So how does heredity fit in with the reincarnation process? Traditionally, heredity is the belief that we are born as a product of our parents simply with the traits they have passed on to us genetically. To the modern reincarnationist, this is only a partial answer. Yes, genetics does have an influence, in that it gives the individual a predisposition to certain traits and characteristics. The reincarnationist, though believes that this is not always by accident. Because of what may need to be learned on a soul level, because of what has been accomplished in the past, we choose parents and environments who can give us this predisposition.

The thing we must keep in mind is that there is always a free variable involved in the process. We cannot know everything that will unfold. We cannot control all the elements of our rebirth and its environment. We will have free will and so will everyone else upon the planet. We can choose and set the outline for our life circumstances, but the details within that outline can change entirely from what we may anticipate. Once we are in the physical, things are not predestined. The soul chooses circumstances that it hopes will provide further growth and development, but not all elements of that rebirth are controllable.

I believe the soul knows this on some level and chooses circumstances of birth that it hopes will lead to positive growth. Because some things are not always foreseeable, changes may need to be made. Even then it recognizes there will be opportunities for growth.

A common argument against reincarnation is that involving victims of child abuse. Were they abusers in a previous life? What are they going to learn from such circumstances? Why would any soul place itself within that kind of situation? Unfortunately, this is where that variable of free will enters.

The study of reincarnation and past lives can help us to see patterns beyond the immediate. They can help us to become more responsible within our choices, whether it is the choice to have a child or the choice to behave in a certain manner. Before we can change a behavior effectively, we must root out its source. We must begin to see that our physical lifetime is but a fraction in the life of the soul. We must realize that our present personality is a synthesis of all the personalities we have had and developed in all lives. We manifest one personality which is being evolved, but it is an aggregation of the essential elements from all of the previous ones.* We live and express ourselves in an infinite number of ever-changing moments. They are all connected, but each is also unique unto itself.

---

*In the phenomena of multiple personality disorders, experiments and research is being done from a past life perspective. The trauma of abuse, common to those of this disorder, is believed to splinter that synthesized personality. Thus for each difficult situation that arises, a new splinter occurs and a personality from a past life arises. This personality is usually one that is capable of handling the particular situation.

We reincarnate so that we can build the character of our personalities to a greater, higher degree so that we can fully unite them in harmony with the soul. Through this linking and development we learn to express the energies and force of the soul. We have the opportunity to become the Masters of Evolution, individuals who are co-creators in the world through the powers of love and will.

EXERCISE:
HAVE YOU EXPERIENCED PAST LIVES?

The following list of questions is designed to help you open your mind to the possibility of past life experiences. These are common questions, which, if answered in the affirmative, can be explained through reincarnation. Though there are other possible explanations as well, these can provide clues to possible past life existences. Keep an open mind.

1. Are there places you have always dreamt of visiting?

2. Are there places you would never want to visit?

3. Are there periods of history with which you felt more kinship and which you enjoyed studying more?

4. Are there any activities you have always especially liked to watch or participate in?

5. Are there activities you have always wanted to participate in? Wanted to avoid participating in?

6. Are there areas of the country that you feel negative about?

7. Is there an area of the country you feel especially drawn to?

8. Are there any particular people(s) that

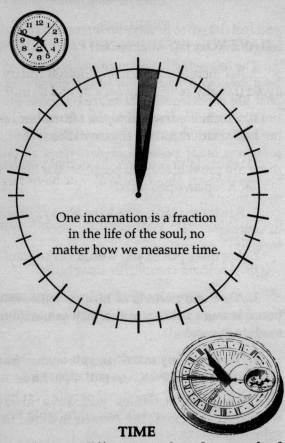

One incarnation is a fraction
in the life of the soul, no
matter how we measure time.

TIME

**Time takes on a different meaning when examined
from the aspect of reincarnation and past lives. One
incarnation is but a fraction of our true lifetime. We
try and measure time in a variety of ways: seconds,
minutes, hours and years, but these measurements
are all geared to a single incarnation. When will we
look beyond?**

you feel drawn to or have an interest in (racially, religiously, socially and so on)?

9. Are there any particular people(s) you try to avoid (racially, religiously, socially and so on)?

10. Are there fears that you remember having had your entire life, since childhood?

11. What talents do you have that you have always known about, even if you have never used them?

12. What are you favorite foods? Least favorite?

13. Are there chronic ills since birth?

14. Are there any chronic problems, emotional issues or attitudes that you can attribute to early childhood?

15. Are there some people you have instantly felt close to, even if you have not known them long? Are there people you have been repelled by or felt uncomfortable with, even if you have just met them?

16. Have you ever experienced a feeling of déjà vu? (Déjà vu comes from the French and means "already seen." This is the experience of recognizing a scene, a street, a house, and so on as being strangely familiar, even though it has never been seen before.)

17. Young children often offer spontaneous evidence of past lives.* They frequently mention other "homes" and other relationships with those around them. These expressions are usually casual and matter of fact. Did you do this as a child? Have you heard other children do so?

18. Can you see where the possibility of past lives would explain the phenomena of child prodigies?

19. Have you ever had recurring dreams of a particular place or time? (Dreams that reflect past lives often recur, and they have a vivid reality about them.) Is an unknown language ever spoken within the dream? Are the characters and setting in the past? Is there an anachronistic element within a modern scene; i.e., clothing, tools and so on from the past?

20. Have you ever had an out-of-body experience, consciously or not? What of a near-death experience? What could these tell you about the possibility of life after death and rebirth?

---

*Such expressions in children is more reliable than with adults. With adults there is a greater possibility of it reflecting information the adult has been exposed to but simply forgotten. In young children this is much less likely, as is the possibility that it is simply the product of an overactive imagination.

2

Awakening Ancient Knowledge of Past Lives

One of the most common complaints voiced by individuals who do not accept or believe in reincarnation is that "everyone seems to have been famous or glamorous in a previous life." Most followers of reincarnation and past lives do not make such claims. Yes, there are those who do, and unfortunately these are the ones who get the attention. Even today, it is not unusual to find a number of individuals who believe they were once Merlin or Nefertiti or King Arthur.

There is, of course, that possibility—in some very rare cases. It is much more likely that we will never know who these historical personalities are in the present—if they are even *in* the present. Most past lives, on the contrary, are boring. Not everyone will remember famous lives. Our greatest growth comes through those lives in which we learn the creative possibilities within the limitations of those circumstances.

It is easy to become too involved in the glamour and wonder of who we were. Past life discovery can be exciting, but we must be careful about creating lifetimes of drama and glamour as a way of compensating for our present life circumstances. We must be pragmatic. When working with past life discovery, it is not as important to be able to demonstrate who we were as it is to learn how that life or series of lives is influencing us now.

Remember that names and dates, even if shown to be authentic and historically correct, do not necessarily prove reincarnation. Nor do they prove that you were the individual who was living at that time. If such information increases our awareness, it has then served a purpose. Reincarnation can only make sense when we view it and experience it as a spiralling evolutionary process—not just a cyclic recurrence.

Knowledge of past lives can assist you in opening to new depths within your own psychological makeup. It can provide greater insight into your present circumstances. It is also not necessary for all people. Some should not waste their time. Their problems exist more in relation to present life causes than to the past. There are also those who have reached a point within their own evolutions and have developed spiritual disciplines strong enough to enlighten and strengthen them increasingly. In these cases the knowledge of past lives is irrelevant.

Remember, too, that you do not have to be aware of the laws of evolution, reincarnation and karma to fulfill yourself and grow. Any human being who lives simply by the golden rule of "doing unto others," who seeks to fulfill his or her duties and obligations in life as creatively as possible, is doing what he or she is supposed to be doing anyway. Living such a live will automatically bring about opportunities to override the influences of the past and sow powerful seeds for the future.

There are many theories about the source of past life information. The first is that we lead a series of lives, each adding to our overall growth and development, and all of the information from those previous lives is stored within the bank of knowledge in a deep level of the mind. A second theory is that we are all multidimensional. In this theory, you are living all of your lives simultaneously, but you are more consciously focused upon your current one. The past life information comes from connecting with those other dimensions of yourself that have chosen different times and scenarios to learn specific lessons.

A third theory about the source for past life knowledge is that our own subconscious translates our current situation, attitudes, events and people into a scenario that will enable us to view them more objectively and gain greater insight into them. The past life uncovered is an intuitive and creative reinterpretation of the present.

A fourth theory is that our own individual soul is part of a greater and grander Oversoul. There can be millions of souls upon the earth that are part of this same Oversoul. When we access what we believe to be past life information, we are simply tapping into that bank of experiences shared and lived by other souls that are linked to the same Oversoul. This concept of the Oversoul can be likened to fantasy role playing. The Oversoul creates characters who participate in adventures in a world that it creates. Each of these characters has a spark of the Oversoul within it, and, at the time of death, that spark and the accumulated knowledge and experience are reassimilated by the Oversoul.*

Yet another theory is that the past life is symbolic of a desire, a wish or even a subconscious prompting to a course of action. For example, an individual who uncovers a past life scenario as Shakespeare may be reflecting a desire to write. Someone who uncovers a past life as a successful gladiator may be getting a message from the subconscious to stand strong and fight harder in some present life situation.

---

*This is similar to the process of the creation of a "tulpa" in Tibet. The practitioners visualize an entity so strongly that it becomes charged and takes on a life of its own. This is accomplished much as an author would create a character, only the level of concentration and the magical ritual surrounding it intensifiy its manifestation. This can be likened also to the materializations experienced in spiritualist seances.

There are other theories as well, but these in themselves should tell us that past life information can not be interpreted simply. Psychology is not an exact science; many aspects of the mind and its functioning are still a complete mystery.

Uncovering past lives works best if approached with the attitude that they are a fact. The interpreting of those "facts" can come later. It is important first to stir the mind into new revelations. Even if we treat them as nothing more than symbolic communications from the subconscious mind, we can open ourselves to tremendous insights. It won't take long to realize that the scenes experienced are more than mere memories of subtle information you have just consciously forgotten.

In the chapters that follow are step-by-step exercises to assist you in your own discovery process. If followed through and approached with the proper attitude, they will elicit dynamic results. The exercises are designed to awaken the deeper levels of consciousness and your creative imagination. Do not confuse creative imagination with that which is all fancy and unreal. It is that power of the human mind which helps us to connect with the subtler realms of our minds and the universe.

The exercises in the rest of the book involve specific meditative techniques, self-hypnosis and dowsing processes that you can use to uncover those lives most affecting you at present. Do not be afraid to adapt them. Also do not enter into them with preconceived notions. Uncovering past lives can shatter many of our expectations and illusions about ourselves. It is a process of self-knowledge and awareness. Use discrimination. Don't always accept the experience literally. Ask constantly how this uncovered lifetime is affecting you now. If that cannot be discerned, the lifetime may simply be a delusion, or irrelevant.

Remember that your primary focus is to always be in the present! If you find yourself constantly talking about your past life experiences or rushing home each night to uncover more, exciting information, or if you find yourself neglecting anything in your present life, stop immediately! You are dealing with subtle levels of the mind, and care must always be taken.

I used to hear in various circles that one should never try to uncover the past because it could draw you away from the present and even splinter your present, synthesized personality. It could reawaken and manifest darker aspects that had already been balanced. They warned that, when it was time to uncover a past life experience, it would reveal itself in its own way. To uncover it before you were ready might reveal past aspects of your character that could frighten you. It could reveal things about you that you would not wish to know.

Yes, any self-discovery process is scary, but if we wish to take control of our lives more consciously and set new patterns, we must be able to identify those old patterns at their roots. Only then can we fully weed our lives. There *are* safe ways of doing this. Remember that discrimination and discernment are the keys. Don't jump to conclusions—positive or negative. At the very least, approach the experiences as symbolic rather than literally as past lives. This will ease you into a fuller understanding until you are ready to grasp the deeper import of the revelation.

Keep an open mind. Remember that the primary commandment of the ancient mystery temples was *"Know thyself!"* Taking responsibility for your own growth and awareness means that you open yourself to life on many levels of existence. Being responsible means that you take what you can find from whatever source you can find—extract it, reshape it and then synthesize it into a system of perpetual growth that works for you as an individual. It is using what you learn and experience in the manner that is best for you. The recognition of this and the creative use of it is makes the wonder and magic of life—past, present and future.

EXERCISE:
KEEPING A PAST LIFE JOURNAL

It is not unusual to experience past life flashes as you begin to exercise the mind and open the exploration process. A good way of recording such flashes and stimulating even more is through the use of a journal. Doing something tangible, such as recording your experiences with the exercises in this book, serves to send a strong message to the subconscious mind. It will realize that you truly are serious about opening those ancient doors. The recording reinforces the message to those deeper levels of the subconscious mind.

Each time you perform one of the exercises, record the effects. What did you experience? What feelings were stirred up? You will also find that, as you record your efforts, you will be rewarded with memories of events from childhood or later that may provide supporting evidence for a past life. Although at the time such events may have seemed inconsequential and were easily dismissed, you will find a number of them lending support to your past life explorations.

A good way of stimulating the subconscious memory and opening those creative doors is through an activity that I often used when I was teaching. I would give a writing assignment to my students at the beginning of the year. It served several purposes: (1) it stimulated their creative juices; (2) it stretched the mind, cleaning the cobwebs out, and (3) it provided me with some wonderful insights into their characters. It is especially effective for loosening up the distant memories of the past—in this life and in previous ones.

Begin your journal with a story about your past. Make it up entirely. Choose an area of the world you have always been fascinated with. Choose a period of time. Now write a fictional account of the sort of person you would have been. In your description, answer the following questions:

1. Would you be a male or a female?

2. What did you do for a living?

3. What kind of clothes or costumes did you wear?

4. What was your house like? What kind of furnishings did you have?

5. What was a normal day in your life like there?

6. What were some of the customs of this area? Were there any unusual ones?

7. Were you married? If so, did you have any children? If not, why not?

8. What kind of laws existed at this time in this place?

9. What were the predominant religious beliefs?

10. Were there ever any special celebrations, religious or otherwise, that you can describe?

Don't be afraid to be creative, and do not worry about historical accuracy. Describe these aspects in as much detail as you can, especially the clothing, customs and the living conditions. Note any particular feelings or emotions that you have about the various things that you describe. Take your time in writing this. Do not rush it. Make sure you are relaxed and undisturbed. Don't worry about style or spelling or grammar. What is most important is the flow of ideas and the descriptions.

It is important for you to imagine what it would be like to live in that place at that time. Don't use reference books. At this point we are simply trying to open those levels of the subconscious mind which house all the memories of all past lives.

I always had some students who would complain they didn't have any imagination and couldn't imagine having lived before. I would tell these individuals to choose a place they would like to visit and live. I would then prompt them with questions: "How would you support yourself there?" "What do you think the people are like?" "How will you be treated?" and so on. Remember the purpose is to not strain, but to let the images and possibilities unfold naturally. You aren't going to be graded on this; it is for your eyes and personal awareness alone.

An interesting phenomena usually occurs in an exercise such as this. As you work and become involved with the description, you will become unaware of the passage of time. Outside sounds will seem to turn off or become very distant. You will become absorbed in the exercise and still be alert. This is part of the right-brain function that will be covered in more detail later in this book. The right hemisphere of the brain assists us in bypassing our normal perceptions of time.

There is an old cliche of how minutes can seem like hours and hours like minutes. Through past life exploration, we learn that we are not at the mercy of time, but only our perception of it. The mind can surmount confinement in space and time.

EXERCISE:
THE WHEEL OF LIFE EXERCISE

This exercise will help you to understand the significance and the ties of the past to the present and the present to the future. It can even be adapted to set the wheels of your own life in motion in a new direction.

The wheel of life is sometimes referred to as the wheel of fortune, which is depicted in a deck of tarot cards. As with all wheel images, it represents a mixed bag of energies. The tarot card and its imagery can be used in meditation to help you see the rise and fall of the patterns within your life and their connections to the past. It can be used to open doors to those times best for awakening fame and fortune and the modern application of ancient knowledge.

The Wheel of Fortune is the card of time. It teaches the importance of synchronicity. It teaches that we each have our own unique rhythm. It teaches how to recognize that rhythm and harmonize it with the grander rhythms of the universe. The energies associated with this card can teach us that seeds do not grow unless planted, and everything that manifests has a gestation and root-forming period before the manifestation and growth is revealed.

The exercise using this tarot image can begin the process of revealing patterns of the past so that they are not repeated in the future. It also creates choices, choices that set the patterns for the future.

This is an exercise which teaches the flow and flux of time and attuning to the rhythms of the universe. As you learn to work with this exercise and adapt its imagery, you will be learning to ride the wheel of life, not as a roulette wheel, but as a wheel that spirals higher and higher with less and less chance of failure. This exercise can reveal the significance and source of those limbo periods in your life while revealing the creative possibilities for moving out of them.

The tarot deck, especially the Major Arcana, is a powerful teaching tool. Hidden within its imagery are the lessons and laws of physical and spiritual phenomena. When we meditate upon these cards, we align ourselves with the energies reflected by them. We set them in motion within our life. By learning to use the images in meditation and concentrated focus, we loosen the restrictions of the mind. Any creative person, artist or inventor has already learned to do so. We are learning to use the imagination in a productive manner.

When you meditate upon the image of the Wheel of Life, you align yourself with those archetypal forces that teach and manifest the energies of rhythm, time and unfoldment. Its image is linked to the archetypal forces of honor and fame and their rise and fall within our lives. Inherent within it are the teachings of the rhythms and patterns of nature and life. It awakens sensi-

THE WHEEL OF FORTUNE
(Rider-Waite Deck)

tivity to the creative energies that have been developed in the past and are inherent in the present—even if unexpressed.

1. Choose a time in which you will not be disturbed. Make sure the phone is off the hook and that there will be no interruptions.

2. Remove the Wheel of Fortune card from a tarot deck of your choosing. Look upon the picture. You may even wish to read about some of its spiritual significance and the correspondences traditionally associated with it.

3. Make sure that you can visualize (image) the card with your eyes closed. Remember that all aspects of the card are designed to help awaken and amplify the archetypal energies of time associated with it. As you concentrate and employ the image through meditation, the play of those archetypal energies of time are released more strongly into your life.

4. Perform a progressive relaxation. Take your time with this. The more relaxed you are, the more able you will be to open to those deeper levels of the subconscious mind. Focus on each part of your body and mentally send warm, soothing energies to it. You may also wish to perform slow, rhythmic breathing. Inhale through your nose for a count of four. Hold for a count of four, and then exhale out your mouth for a count of four.

5. You may wish to employ some soft music and incense to assist you with this. An incense made with a combination of sage and thyme is very effective.

6. Remember that this exercise is also designed to help you learn to use the creative imagination in a productive manner. As with all things, persistence is the key and will bring rewards. Do not be discouraged if there are no immediately recognizable results. They will come. The energies of the archetype to which we align ourselves will play subtly upon us. They may bring specific revelations about patterns of our life that have carried over from previous ones. They may affect our dreams, or they may intensify the effects of the actual past life meditations and regressions found in other parts of the book.

7. Take time at the end of the exercise to write in your Past Life Journal the impressions and feelings you experienced. Take time afterwards to reflect on some of the major patterns within your life. Do they define themselves more clearly? Can you see any patterns in relation to your family? Your work? The kinds of individuals that come into your life? Remember that past life therapy is a process first of self-awareness. We must first recognize patterns and the source of those patterns if we are to change them or amplify them.

8. This exercise is designed to stretch your mind and limber up your subconscious. Only if you loosen your subconscious will you be able to more consciously access it for past life information. The exercise is also designed to increase your personal awareness of time patterns in your life. It is effective to perform this exercise in conjunction with all of the other exercises in this book. Don't perform it on the same day as one of the other exercises, though; rather use it the day before you begin your concentrated past life work with the other exercises. In this way, it becomes an excellent warmup.

9. This exercise will also enhance any past life exploration you have undertaken throughout the year if you perform it at important natural time changes within the yearly cycle. The points at the changes of the seasons and at the major phases of the moon (new and full) are powerful vortices of energy. This exercise helps to activate them specifically to assist you in identifying larger time patterns and rhythms operating within your life. It also plants the seeds that will facilitate specific past life explorations should they be undertaken during that particular cycle (be it seasonal or monthly). When used with the rhythms of nature, it should be performed three days in a row—the day before, the day of and the day after the lunar phase or equinox/solstice.

10. When used periodically throughout the year, whether as warmup to the other past life work or as a way of attuning to the changing rhythms of nature, it will increase your overall sensitivity to the past foundations that are affecting your present. It will help you to recognize past connections more easily. Even if you cannot discern all of the details, you will still be able to recognize that there truly is a past link with this person, that situation, these attitudes and so on. As a result, you will be able to handle it all more constructively.

The Wheel of Life

As you relax, imagine that you hear a clock chiming softly in the background. It chimes 12 times and then fades. As it fades,you see forming before you a large, ancient wooden door. Carved and painted into the door is the exact image of the tarot card, the Wheel of Fortune.

You are standing before the door. It softly opens outward, spilling beautiful purple and blue lights out and around you. You are surrounded by the colors of rich deep blues and purples. The light spirals around and around, drawing you through the doorway. Again you hear a distant clock chiming softly. As you step through over the threshold, the door closes behind you.

You are standing in a sea of blue and purple spirals. Against that backdrop of spirals, you see a sun shining upon a tree. As you look at that tree, you see how it reflects the passing of the seasons. As the sun moves across the sky, the leaves begin to bud. Then they turn a rich green, only to be painted with the colors of autumn and then fall to earth. The bare limbs of the tree are then covered with snow. Then the snow melts, revealing the first buds of spring. Spring, summer, autumn and winter. One season passes into another. One year after another. They all follow the same pattern. They all have the same rhythm and cycle. Over and over again.

Then the image of the sun and tree fade in the mist of blue and purple spirals of energy. In the place where the sun used to be, the moon rises. It shifts from new to full and back to new. Every phase of the moon is revealed for you, over and over again and then is lost within the purple spirals of light.

The distant chiming becomes even more distinct. As it does, the scenery shifts again, becoming more distinct. The sky and the earth are filled with shades of blue and purple. It seems as if you have found a void in which everything upon the earth rests in limbo. Above you now are both the sun and the moon. Covering the earth are clocks of all shapes and sizes: grandfather clocks, cuckoo clocks, watches . . . They hang upon trees and are encased in stone. The entire landscape is surreal.

You move closer to the clocks. On some, the hands turn clockwise, clicking off the minutes with great speed. You step toward one and you feel and see yourself aging. You can actually feel your hair growing and wrinkles forming. You step back quickly, feeling your face, reassuring yourself that you are no older than you were before.

On some clocks, the hands spin counter-clockwise. You step toward them, and you feel your energy growing. You feel younger, stronger, more vibrant. Your skin is smooth, and your hand, as you hold it up to your face, is very soft and childlike. You feel yourself growing smaller, becoming a child again. You jump back, touching yourself and examining your hands to make sure you are who you were.

Some of the clocks spin round and round, never stopping. Some seem not to move at all. As you look upon them, you see that episodes of your life are shown in the face of each clock. Some reflect the seasons of learning. Some reflect the patterns of relationships. Some reflect moments of exquisite joy, and others reflect agonizing, long minutes of worry. Some reflect scenes that are strange and exotic and yet somehow familiar. And you know these reflect past incarnations.

Within these timepieces are the patterns and rhythms of your entire lifetime, not just one incarnation. Only as you bring them all into harmony does true enlightenment occur. Only as you learn to move the hands of time in synchronicity do your luck and fortune change.

You begin to touch the clocks and, with your

fingertips, you force the hands of several clocks to move in unison. You guide the hands, slowing some down and speeding others up. As you do, a breath of fresh air blows, caresses you softly, acknowledging a new harmony.

You look about you. There are so many clocks, so many rhythms. There is so much to do. Then you realize that, as you learn to harmonize your rhythms with those of the universe, you will have all the time in the world.

With this realization, you are aware of the deep chiming of a distant clock again. It is as if the great timepiece of the universe were chiming your perception. You raise your eyes to the heavens and you see the sun and moon blending together. It thrills you and excites you. It reminds you that all is possible in time.

The images of the clocks fade and the blue and purple spirals dance strongly. You turn and see that the door through which you entered is again open. You step through aware that time is always open to you. The door closes softly and gently, closing off the spirals of energy. You see the painted image on the face of the door. You now know that it is not truly a Wheel of Fortune but rather the Wheel of Life!

The image of the door fades softly, dissipating before your eyes. You breathe deeply, relaxed and remembering all that you have experienced. Record this experience in your Past Life Journal.

3

Understanding the Role of Karma

You are energy. You are energy that uses the garment of a physical body to learn and to grow. In the reincarnation process, your true essence works with three predominant principles in that growth and education.

The first is simply the principle of evolution. Your essence is born under conditions which will provide opportunities for the development of the qualities and characteristics you are most in need of. These conditions provide opportunities for increasing and progressive change. The framework for this change and growth is set through heredity, the time and conditions of birth (astrological and terrestrial) and environmental factors that can influence you and assist you in achieving the necessary growth. These environmental factors include such things as race, religion, sex, family, friends, acquaintances and other associations and possible experiences likely to be encountered.

The second principle is free will. We all have the freedom to make choices, take actions, make decision or not. We are not bound to fulfill what we have come to fulfill. It is true that once we have taken physical form, some factors cannot be changed. We can't change our race, hereditary traits, some congenital problems and so on. For this reason an old axiom is often given in conjunction with the principle of free will: "What can't be cured, must be endured." There are some aspects that free will cannot override. On the other hand, we have great latitude in the choices and courses of action we take within the framework of our life environs.

The third principle is the one most important and often misunderstood aspect of reincarnation. It is the principle of karma. Within this principle operates what is sometimes called the Law of Compensation or the Law of Equilibrium. How you have used your free will in the past helps determine the life outline of conditions, situations, opportunities and environment that will provide the most beneficial learning and growth. You can predestine aspects of your fate by your actions, whether those actions be thoughts, feelings, words or deeds.

This principle of karma has been expressed in various ways. In the Christian tradition, we see it as, "Whatsoever a man soweth, that shall he also reap." In physics it is the principle that every action has an equal but opposite reaction. What you put out, you get back. "What goes around, comes around." For every cause there is an effect; for every effect there is a cause.

Karma is a Sanskrit word which means "to do or to make." It is energy in action. Everything we do or make provides an opportunity for growth. Because of this, we do not want to look at karma as simply a process of debts and balances. Many times we choose an incarnation that can be more trying and testing to help us learn specific lessons needed on a soul level. When we make right decisions and actions, positive and rewarding opportunities open their doors. They are not necessarily handed to us on a silver platter, but the doors are opened. If we make wrong choices or actions, these in turn create their own consequences.

Being responsible requires that we consciously make our choices, knowing these choices will bring about certain consequences. We may hope they come out a certain way, but, if we are truly responsible, we must be willing to take the consequences—good, bad or indifferent—knowing we will learn from them.

It is not unusual for many to blame everything that goes wrong on "bad karma." Usually these individuals are confusing bad karma with bad judgment. Not everything is a result of past actions. Yes, there may be a certain outline of life environs and circumstances that is the result of the past, but within that outline we are developing new abilities and creativity. We are encountering new growth opportunities. Many lessons simply revolve around recognizing our opportunities and making the correct choices.

Traditionally there have been considered to be three expressions of karma within life, but there are actually many variations of these:

The first is the *boomerang expression*. In this kind of situation, if we have hurt another, we in turn are hurt. If we have helped another person, we will find ourselves in a position where another will help us.

The second is the *organism expression*. If you abused another physically, such as causing another's blindness, you may in turn be born blind. If you helped one with blindness, you in turn may be born with even better eyesight.

The third is *symbolic karmic expression*. If you constantly turned a deaf ear to others in a lifetime, you may be born with hearing problems. If you look for the good in others, you may be born with heightened intuition and perception.

Karma is learning, and anything you do provides opportunity for such, whether it is something from the past or something new entirely. There is compensation that plays within this principle of karma, but it is not revengeful. If you did something wrong in a past life, it does not mean that you must have that something done to you in the present. An exaggerated example is in the case of murder. If you murdered someone in the past, it does not mean that you have to come back and be murdered. Karma is not an "eye for an eye" process.

In the above example, the individual who committed the murder may come back into a life situation in which he or she must learn to handle the anger and violence in another way. This situation could be something such as being the primary support for the other individual— a parent or benefactor, for example. It could also mean coming back into a situation in which the murderer is placed within life circumstances that will strongly ingrain the negative aspects of anger and violence. It could also mean coming back into a similar kind of situation to provide an opportunity to make the correct choice.

We each learn our lessons differently because we are each at our own level of growth. The consequences will vary from individual to individual. Within one lesson there can be many variations and many life situations to provide the most beneficial opportunity for learning. If there has been a misuse of free will, circumstances will unfold so that the soul can learn to use it productively.

The soul does not have to suffer to progress. Suffering is only good for the soul if it teaches us how not to suffer again. The exercise of your free will in conjunction with karma does not have to be painful to have effects. Progress occurs when you move in harmony with the natural laws of the universe. If you have been out of harmony and work to bring yourself back in, the change can bring stress, turmoil and disruption—but only of the old, inharmonious patterns. As they are removed, the new, instigated harmony prevails and opportunity for success and reward increases.

Karma is constructive, with its aim as guidance. It seeks only adequate adjustment of conditions. It teaches us that we cannot separate ourselves from others. There are ties that go beyond time and space. In many societies of the Native American tradition, decisions were not made until consequences were examined as far ahead as seven generations. They recognized the intimate and intricate tie between all people and all situations.

Karma will select a time for compensation when the individual will benefit the most by the lesson being learned and at a time in which it can be utilized most effectively. The place of compensation occurs where it is most favorable for a demonstration to all who can profit by it. Its means of compensating will vary to suit the greatest consideration for all living creatures. Karma unfolds in the time, manner and means that is best for us if we allow it to do so. This doesn't mean that we should sit back and do nothing. Rather, we make our choices and take our actions and then allow the consequences to unfold so we can determine new choices and new courses of action.

Karma does not necessarily seek retribution. Its goal is learning and growth. It exacts an adjustment of conditions, a balancing or even just a realization. It can even be suspended upon a physical level if there is a true emotional, mental and spiritual compensation. Self-control, hard work, love and acceptance, wisdom and grace are the means to overcome any karmic problem. Learning to see the creative possibilities that exist within our limitations opens us to the positive aspects of karmic growth.

It is as easy to be unmindful of things that can set karma in motion as it is to not recognize the effects of our karma. For example, we may have earned the blessing of health and be so unappreciative of it that we take it for granted and neglect it, undoing what we have already accomplished. We must always build.

Our karmic responsibility—our learning—increases as we become more responsible for our growth and our daily trials and obligations. In true discipleship, we take on our karmic learning at an accelerated rate. We may take on the difficult lessons of a dozen lifetimes within a single one. The task is to remain creative enough to produce good effects and to endure the intensity, while still remaining productive and beneficial for humanity.

If we are to begin a process of becoming more responsible for our learning, we must recognize that there are many types of karma or learning available to us. Family karma, racial karma, religious karma, national karma, world karma and of course our own personal karma all play a factor in our growth.

Family and business relationships are usually our most karmic. They provide our greatest opportunities for growth. There are other lessons that we encounter as well, depending upon our race, religion and nationality. Because of this, we incarnate as different sexes, races, nationalities and so on to round out our universal life experiences. For example, all who live in the United States must learn lessons in the proper use of freedom. In this country we often see extremes of too much freedom or too many restrictions. Learning the proper expression of freedom requires discipline, and everyone in this country works with it on some level. It is part of our national karma.

We must begin to see that everything and everyone in our lives has a greater significance than we have ever imagined. Past life exploration helps us with this. We begin to see the spiritual behind the physical, and our lives open to new expressions.

EXERCISE:
SEEING KARMIC CONNECTIONS

The following story is drawn from the many old Hassidic tales about Rabbi Israel, the Baal Shem Tov. Baal Shem Tov means "Master of the Wondrous Name." This particular story is adapted from the book *Classic Hassidic Tales* by Meyer Levin (New York: Dorset Press, 1959). It is an excellent story for shedding light on the intricasies of karmic links. Studying it and meditating upon it can assist you in realizing that our ties to other people within our lives may have origins far beyond what we have ever imagined.

Two Souls

(The mystery of two souls that were separated and how Rabbi Israel brought them together when they suffered rebirth on earth.)

The Baal Shem Tov said, "From every human being there rises a light that reaches straight to heaven. And when two souls that are destined to be together find each other, their streams of light flow together, and a single brighter light goes forth from their united being."

Every year an old woman made a pilgrimage to Rabbi Israel to ask him for prayers that she might bear a child. Rabbi Israel knew though that no child was yet to be born through her, and he always told her to go home and wait.

Year by year she grew older and more bent, but she always made the pilgrimage to Rabbi Israel. One year, though, he said to her, "Go home. This year a child will be given to you."

He never saw the old woman in the next five years, and Rabbi Israel knew she had had her child. In the fifth year, he saw her again, with a small child by her side.

She told the Rabbi she loved the child but could not keep him. She said that his soul was not kin to her. He was a gentle boy and obedient, but his eyes shown with a wisdom that she could not bear.

The Rabbi took the child and raised him, and he was soon the best scholar in the area. Many wealthy people came to the Rabbi to arrange a marriage, but always the Rabbi refused. Instead he sent to a distant village for the third daughter of a poor farmer.

This daughter was the quietest of the farmer's children. She was good and gentle. The farmer agreed to the marriage and brought his daughter to Rabbi Israel. There they were received with great honor. A feast was prepared, and the Baal Shem Tov read the service of the marriage and blessed the new husband and wife.

When the ceremony was over and they all sat to eat, the Rabbi rose and said, "I will now tell a story." And everyone knew this would be no ordinary story.

"Long ago," he said, "there was a king who fretted that he had no heir. Not even the sorcerers and wise men were able to help. Then one of his wizards presented an idea to the King.

" In your land there are many Jews, and they have a powerful God. Forbid them to worship, under pain of death, until a son is born.'

"This the king did, and darkness came over the land. Many fled the kingdom. Others worshiped in secret. Others hid their own sons, for it was the king's decree that no child would be circumcised until his heir was born. If a child was found circumcised, the king's soldiers would cut the child in two with their swords.

"Many children were slaughtered and the people of the land were filled with grief. The angels on high saw the suffering and raised their voices in song beseeching God to send a son. Then one soul, purer than the rest, one who had been freed from the earthly bonds, stepped forward and offered to suffer again the *gilgul*, the reincarnation. This he offered that the suffering might cease.

"God consented, and when the child was born, the King forgot about the Jews. But the laws were not withdrawn. The prince grew to be beautiful and skilled in learning. The son was provided with every luxury, but he seemed to take no pleasure in it, and even as a child he drained the knowledge from all the wise men of the kingdom. But the son was discontent.

"The king searched for a wise man to teach his son happiness. After many days he found an aged man who was willing to teach the prince. The old man agreed on the condition that he be allowed to have a chamber in which he would not be disturbed by anyone for one hour each day. This the king gladly decreed.

"The prince was happy with his new teacher; they explored new depths of wisdom. One day, though, the prince followed the old man into the chamber and saw him standing before an altar. There he discovered that the old man was a rabbi who worshiped, in spite of the laws of the kingdom. The young boy did not care, for the wisdom to be touched was yet too great. He begged the rabbi to teach him even more. After much begging, the rabbi agreed on the condition it be far away from the kingdom.

"They left, and for years the young prince grew in his scholarship. He became celebrated among the rabbis for his wisdom. Still he was discontent, for though he had knocked on the innermost door of heaven, it had remained closed to him. A hand had shown him a blot upon his soul.

"Then one day he met the daughter of a rabbi, and her soul quivered. As the young prince looked upon her, he knew she would be the end of his loneliness. So the two were married, and so true was the love of their souls that, at the moment of their marriage, a single light streamed upward to heaven and lighted the whole world.

"The soul of the prince had learned to leave the body to rise to the heavens and return with greater wisdom. After one such moment, he looked upon his wife and spoke softly. `This night I pierced to the highest heavens. I learned that my soul was born in sin. I was raised in luxury and ignorance while the people of my kingdom suffered. For that I cannot attain perfection. There is only one thing I can do. I may consent to immediate death, and afterwards my soul must be reborn through a pure but humble woman, and the first years of my life must be passed in poverty. Only in that next incarnation may I attain perfection.'

"The wife agreed only on the condition that she be able to die with him and then be reborn, to become his wife and be one with him again. To this he agreed.

"They lay down together, and their souls went forth in the same breath. For timeless ages the souls strayed in the darkness. And at last the soul of the boy returned to be born as the son of an old woman. And the soul of the girl returned to earth to be born as the third daughter of a poor farmer.

"And so all the days of their childhood and youth were a seeking for they knew not what. Their hearts yearned and their eyes looked with hope toward each new soul, until they forgot what they awaited."

Rabbi Israel paused in his story and looked at the celebrants around the table. "Know my friends that these two souls have at last found each other again and have come together today as husband and wife."

Then the master was silent, and all felt a joy fill them. The young man and the young woman held hands, and their eyes were lighted by a single flame that rose to the heavens.

4

Karmic Connections, Soul Mates and Twin Souls

Nothing is so fascinating as uncovering the past life connections we have had with others who are in our present life. As a general rule, the people with whom we have our strongest emotional ties were usually connected to us in some form in a past life. Souls who are closely related in one lifetime often meet in others. Their roles may change from life to life, but the connection remains. Since we help choose the life environments in which we can grow from where we left off in the previous life, it is not unreasonable to believe that we would choose to be reborn with those who are closest to us.

If the relationship was one of love, the love will persist and have an opportunity to deepen under new life circumstances. If the connection was one of enmity, circumstances may be chosen so as to provide the opportunity to overcome it. Often, if there is an obligation, circumstances may be chosen to provide opportunities to fulfill it. Keep in mind, though, that there is always free will, and not everything can be controlled once we are reborn into the physical.

All of our relationships are karmic. They provide opportunities for learning. What form that learning takes will vary. In family situations, there is usually a particular, predominant lesson that touches all members. For example, all members of a family may be learning about the lessons involved in properly expressing strength of will. In one member, you may find an extreme case of bullying and domineering. In another member, you may find an individual always giving in. In another member of the family, you may find an individual refusing to follow any orders or suggestions simply because they come from someone else. In yet another, you may see a lack of assertion or an addictive behavior. There are many variations and subtleties in any single lesson. Recognizing the common patterns of behavior among the various family members can reveal much about the karmic lessons you have come to learn through your family.

This understanding can be applied to business and social situations as well. We must look not only for the emotional connections, but also, more importantly, for the subtle and obvious patterns that play out within our relationships. We often see how a childhood experience can set a pattern of behavior for a lifetime. The most obvious example is child abuse, the result of which is often a lifetime of difficulty in personal relationships. Why is it not feasible, then, that a single lifetime can set a pattern that will carry over into other lifetimes as well?

We may never determine for certain who anyone might have been in his or her last existence, nor why she or he is on the earth at this time, but by looking at how we relate to a person, and he or she to us, we can open ourselves to some powerful possibilities. Examine your relationships with those closest to you. What kind of emotions do you feel or frequently express around them? The answer can indicate past life relationships to that other person.

Are you always coming to the aid of others? Maybe you were a law officer in the past. Are you always mothering another person, even if she or he is older? Perhaps you were that person's mother in the past. Are you always teasing? Maybe you were a childhood friend or a brother or sister to this individual. Are you always expecting the other person to protect and nurture you? Maybe he or she was a parent or guardian to you in the past. Are you always looking to the other person for money? This could indicate a past business association.

We learn our greatest lessons through other people. In the study of karma and past lives, there are three levels of relationships.

The Karmic Connection Level

These are individuals with whom we may have shared some general experiences in the past. These experiences can be positive or negative. People that we feel instantly familiar with or take an instant liking or disliking for can fall into this category. These are often brief connections and are not usually meant to be anything else. We may be drawn back into contact with these people again only for brief periods in order to fulfill some aspect of the Law of Compensation.

The difficulty with these connections lies in recognizing them for what they are. It is not unusual to find an instant attraction and connection with someone. Unfortunately, we often jump to wrong conclusions. Often I hear individuals say that they have met someone and that they are positive that the other person must be their soul mate. Then, after several months or several years, after a rocky marriage and a stormy divorce, it is dangerous to remind them of their earlier "soul mate conclusion." Unfortunately, many of these same individuals do it all over again. A pattern is established. The individual in the search for his or her soul mate falls into a cycle of karmic connections. The faces may change but the pattern remains the same.

People complain, "Why do I keep meeting these same kinds of people?" "Why do I always run into these same types of situations?" If we fail to see the patterns, the patterns can't be broken. Such patterns can carry on throughout the lifetime or carry over from one life to the next. Using past life therapy helps us to see our patterns. It helps place them in a scenario in which we can view them more objectively. We can see how we typically respond in these kinds of situations so that we can begin avoiding those incorrect behavior patterns.

Part of the function of a long betrothal period was to insure that the relationship was more than just an instant karmic connection. It enabled the energies of the two people to either grow and establish themselves on a stronger, deeper level or else to dissipate naturally. Many divorces could be avoided if greater time was taken to establish compatibility on more than just a few levels.

The Soul Mate Connection

This is one in which two souls are extremely compatible on most levels. They are physically, emotionally, mentally and spiritually compatible. There are many interests in common. They are most often friends first before anything else. Soul mates are individuals who have incarnated and shared many positive, long-term relationships.

We can have more than one soul mate. In fact, considering how many lifetimes we may have had, it is not unreasonable to assume we have several soul mates. There can be a number of individuals with whom we have shared long, positive lifetime experiences. Soul mates can also be either of the opposite or the same sex. They can be a friend, a family member or a spouse.

Soul mates are individuals with whom we share a long association. It does not have to be a continual one, but it is usually extensive. An individual may pop in and out of our lives periodically over a long period of time. Whenever they do, they bring a sense of wonder and renewal. We enjoy whatever time we may share with them, no matter how brief. They touch our lives positively and we touch theirs.

Like karmic connections, the liking can be instant, although it is not always as passionate. Separating the soul mate connection from the karmic connection is not always easy. Time and the degree of compatibility on all levels are two factors to consider. Question yourself: "Am I as important and intrinsic in all levels to this person's life as he or she is to me?"

Yes, there will be differences, as you both are unique and individual souls, but there will be common ground in regard to your goals and aspirations. Soul mates have a friendship that extends and lasts through all circumstances. In the case of spouses, you will often be friends first before being lovers. There is always a bond of unconditional love and support, and you always think of the other's needs before your own. You strengthen the life of each other, adding new dimensions and new depths of love and joy.

The Twin Soul Connection

There is often much discussion and confusion in metaphysical and spiritual circles about the idea of twin souls. A prominent theory is that the twin soul is our ideal other half. At some point, our soul essence splits in two, each half evolving separately. Then, occasionally, the two souls reconnect in the physical for the express purpose of performing some specific, great mission. This is a common theory that has been channeled and which has gained popularity in recent times. However, it is not a theory that will hold up to strong discrimination and spiritual testing.

If one original soul splits to form two souls, each evolving separately, aren't they independent souls in themselves at this point? Isn't this the same as an egg splitting in the womb of the mother? The result is twins, but each is a unique and individual soul unto itself.

This theory also implies that we only incarnate as a particular sex, and this contradicts the idea that reincarnation serves to teach us all aspects of the evolutionary process. There are some lessons that we can only learn by being reborn as a particular, sex, race and so on. The twin soul theory implies that we only participate in half of the learning process.

The twin soul idea is not a concept that has been taught by masters in the past. Yes, most of them taught reincarnation and karmic connec-

The Twin Soul is not found outside of us. It is the inner part of us that must be united with our outer aspects. The more the two are harmonized, the more we enjoy the magic and wonders of life.

WITHIN YOU

We are each a combination of male and female energies. If we are male, an ideal female half lives within. If we are female, there is an ideal male aspect within. To harmonize and unite both aspects is to create new life for ourselves and those we touch.

tions, but they also taught that the quest for the spiritual did not have to go any further than yourself. *"Know thyself"* was the pre-eminent commandment. They taught that we are all a combination of masculine and feminine energies. Learning to harmonize both within any particular incarnation is the key to true balance and spirituality.

To search the outer world, as many do, for that one ideal other half who thinks, feels, believes, and understands every intimate aspect of yourself leads to great discontent. No one will ever live up to those standards, and insisting on this ideal provides an excuse for not committing to people or situations.

Your ideal half lives within you. It is the inner, ideal male or female to your outer self. As you learn to honor and reverence those aspects associated with both parts of your essence, enlightenment occurs. When you learn to bring together the male and the female within yourself, the Holy Child within is born. A new life and a new cycle of growth opens for you.

We all have an idea of what the ideal male or female would be for us. The people that we are drawn to often reflect some aspect or quality of that ideal. We see within them an outer reflection of the inner part of us that we must bring to life. Those who are our soul mates reflect much of that ideal within us, as we do within them. They are as close as we can get to that ideal through another person. They are reminders of the promise of the spiritual.

How we handle our relationships reflects much about our growth or lack of it. Part of our task is to learn how to make our lives work. Sometimes this requires that we look at them from a completely different perspective. Our karmic links to others are intricate, and we cannot lock them into definite patterns, but everything and everyone we encounter can provide an opportunity for personal knowledge and transcendence. Through knowledge of the past, we can come to understand our present and reshape our future.

EXERCISE:
OPENING THE GALLERY
OF YOUR PAST LIVES

The following meditation is dynamic way of beginning to recognize some of the past life connections between yourself and others that are presently in your life. It is an exercise that can be repeated regularly and adapted to explore various aspects of your past.

The effects of this exercise can be heightened by using the meditational aids that are discussed in the next chapter; i.e., incense, candles, fragrances and so on. The important part is to imagine the scenes as well as you can. Many worry that what they see is all a figment of their imagination and not a real experience. Do not confuse imagination with the unreal. They are often quite different. We could not imagine something if there was not some basis or connection for it.

In this exercise, you may actually see the past life, or you may simply get a feeling or an impression. One is neither better nor worse than the other. However you experience it, it will intensify as you persist. Each time you perform the exercise, you will get more dynamic results. If you have difficulty imaging the scenes, simply ask yourself: "If there is such and such there, what would it look like?" Then trust those impressions.

Remember that we are opening doors that have long been closed. It may take a little prying, but they will open. Do not be discouraged. I have not encountered anyone who has not achieved results with this particular past life meditation by the third performance.

1. Make sure you will be undisturbed. Take the phone off the hook and inform others that may be in the house not to interrupt you. You may do this exercise in a seated or lying position.

2. Use any of the incenses or candle preparations that are described in chapter 5 to help set the atmosphere. You may also wish to play some soft music in the background, but it should not be distracting.

3. Perform some rhythmic breathing. Inhale through your nose slowly for a count of four. Hold your breath for a count of four, then exhale out your mouth slowly for a count of four. Keep your breaths slow, steady and comfortable. Do this for several minutes. It eases any tension and helps to shift the mind from outer activities and its usual focuses to a state in which the inner world can more easily be experienced.

4. Now re-read the exercise. Remember the main ideas. You do not have to hold to the letter of the meditation. Don't be afraid to adapt it, and don't worry if you find that, once in it, your experiences differ from those described. This is simply your own mind responding in the manner best for you. If you wish, you may want to

record the meditation and then, once the preparations are made, follow your own voice through it.

5. Now perform a progressive relaxation. Start at your feet and focus your attention on them. Mentally send warm and relaxing feelings to them. Now move up, focusing on each part of your body in turn. Take your time with this. The longer you take, the more relaxed you will be and the better the results you will get. By the time you end at the top of your head, you should feel very relaxed. Your arms and legs should feel heavy, and you should even feel a little disconnected with yourself.

6. At this point, keep your eyes closed to avoid any visual distractions and allow the scenario of the meditation to unfold within your mind.

7. Pay attention to your dreams for several nights following this meditation (and the others found throughout the rest of this book). Anytime you touch the subconscious strongly, as you will do with these exercises, it will have repercussions in your dream life. This does not mean that you will dream of past lives, although that does happen with some people. Rather pay attention to the primary emotional content of your dreams and who these emotions are associated with in the dream scenarios. This can often indicate the emotions and issues that you have come to deal with in regard to these indi-

viduals. (Performing this exercise before sleep can enhance its effect on your dreams and provide further illumination.)

8. You may wish to use the "Wheel of Life" exercise (pages 29-38) as a prelude to this. If so, perform it the day before you begin the initial series with this exercise. This is the key exercise in past life exploration as detailed within this book. It stretches the creative imagination and it opens the subconscious. Even minimal success with this exercise will facilitate all of the other techniques whether used separately or in conjunction with this one.

If you are truly serious about your past life explorations, "Opening the Gallery" will elicit results. Initially, do this exercise for seven days in a row. Most people get results within the week. Then continue performing the exercise once or twice a week for a month. I have not encountered anyone who has not obtained some past life information during this time. Then simply continue periodically, using it with the other techniques.

9. Once you have opened the "Gallery of Your Life," the other exercises on specific past life explorations within this book will be much easier. This is why it is initially important to perform it for a week and then continue using it several times a week for at least a month afterward. It is especially effective at the time of the full moon. If

you decide to extend your past life explorations over a year, it can be beneficial to perform this exercise around the time of the full moon to keep the doors to the inner gallery open.

10. It can also be used as a prelude to augment the effects of the other past life exploration techniques, particularly the therapy techniques associated with the Tree of Life (chapter 6).

Gallery of Life

You see yourself at the top of a long, golden staircase. It spirals gently down into a mist below. You are not afraid. In fact, you feel a sense of anticipation about that which you are going to uncover.

You begin to descend. With each step, you find yourself becoming more relaxed. Down and down you descend. Softly. Gently. It feels good to step down this staircase.

You find yourself going deeper and deeper, descending further and further. Down. Down. Down. You relax even more deeply with each step. You had forgotten how good it feels just to relax.

The further you descend, the lighter you seem to become. It is as if you are barely touching each step. Lighter and softer, as you descend deeper and deeper. Soon the mist is all about you, but you do not mind it. It is beautiful and soothing. And you have not felt so light and loose for a long time.

You are becoming so relaxed and so light that your are literally floating down the stairs. You feel like a soft cloud descending from the heavens. Below, you see the bottom of the stairwell. The mist begins to dissipate, and very gently your feet touch the floor. You are relaxed and at peace.

You see that you are in the middle of a circular room. Across the room from you is a large oaken door. You feel drawn to it. As you step closer, you see your name engraved into the heart of the door itself. Below your name is an engraving in a language that is foreign to you. You reach out gently with your hand and trace the letters with your fingers. As you do, you know that this is your name as it was the last time you were here.

As you draw your hand back, the door opens inward and blue and gold light streams forth. It encircles you. It passes through you. It surrounds you and embraces you. It invites you across the threshold. You close your eyes and you feel the joy of the light.

You open your eyes and step carefully through the open doorway, across the threshold. As you step across, the door closes softly behind you. The blue and gold light gently fades, and you find yourself in what looks like an old storehouse for an art gallery.

Surrounding you are artifacts from every part of the world. There are sculptures, paintings and articles of clothing. There are books and weapons, carvings and wares. Every time period seems to be represented. You recognize some periods and artifacts, but others are alien and confusing. There are cobwebs and dust on many of them, but you can see that they are all still in good condition.

The room is divided into cubicles and sections. Each area reflects a specific time and place in the history of the world—no, not the world! A realization hits you as you look in the closest cubicle. There are articles of clothing that you recognize from childhood. There is your favorite toy! This is not a gallery of the world, but a gallery of *your life*. These artifacts are the traces of the past that have helped form the person that you are now!

With this realization, the gallery darkens except for a small area to your left. There, a divider, a free standing wall, is illuminated. You move toward it, wondering what you will discover about yourself.

As you step around to the front face of this wall, you see hanging upon it a life-size portrait in a large, gilded frame. The image in the portrait is indistinct, but somehow you know that, when it shows itself, it will be an image of you. And then, within your mind, you hear a soft, clear voice:

"This is the Gallery of Your Life. Within it are the remnants of everything and everyone in your past. Within this gallery is all you will ever need to uncover the rhythms of the past as they play within the present. You can choose to see or not to see, as you desire."

The voice stops, and you stare at the portrait. The image shimmers, and a soft breeze blows across you and the portrait. As it does, the image stands strong and clear. See it. Feel it and know that it is real.

Take a few moments and study the portrait. Notice the sex, the clothes, the colors. As you look upon it, you find that you seem to know about this person. You know whether she or he was rich or poor. You know what his or her occupation was. You know whether this person was happy or sad. The face reveals knowledge that you had forgotten.

You look toward the right-hand bottom corner of the portrait. On the frame itself is a small brass plate. It is engraved with a date. You reach out with your finger and trace the date, feeling each number in turn. You look toward the left-hand corner, and there is a second brass plate. It is engraved with the name of a place. It could be a city, a town, a country. Reach out and touch it with your finger.

As you raise your eyes back toward the face of the image in the portrait, you begin to see two other images forming in the background. One is male and the other female. As you look upon their faces, you know what their relationship was to you in that life, be it friend, lover, or family member. And as you study their faces, you remember the emotions that you associated with them. Take a few moments and allow the images to strengthen.

As you realize who these figures were in your past, their faces blur. They become indistinct, and then they begin to crystallize yet again. But something is different. This time as they crystallize, you see the faces of two individuals within your present life. As their faces become clear, you begin to understand your relationships with them a little better. See it. Feel it. And know that it is real.

Then the faces fade. The only image left is the one that is of you. As you look upon it, the eyes seem to come alive, embracing you. And then there appears a word or a phrase above the head. This is what this past life has given to you to use in the present. See it form and stand strong within the portrait.

As you look upon it, you understand yourself a little better. And then, without warning, the image fades until there is just an empty picture frame upon the wall.

You sigh. There is so much that you still do not understand. There is so much yet to learn and figure out. You step back and notice that the entire gallery is lit once more. It seems to stretch on forever. There is so much to learn, so much to remember.

You turn toward the door. As you pause before it, you hear the voice once more.

"This is *your* gallery. Its door is never closed to you. You may explore that which you have seen today even further, or explore any other lifetime that you choose. As you remember the lessons of the past, you will be able to reshape your future."

The door opens slowly, and the gold and blue light encircles you, embracing and blessing you as you step back across the threshold. As the door closes behind you, you know that it will never be truly closed again. You touch the engraving of your name gently once more and then move to the staircase.

You are relaxed, peaceful and filled with a new sense of wonder. As you ascend the stairs lightly and easily through the mist, you take with you your newfound realization. You will never be able to look upon yourself, or the other two who appeared within the portrait, in quite the same way again. And you are filled with a sense of promise.

5

Understanding and Aiding Past Life Meditation

Much has been written about meditation and the various practices thereof. In fact, there are as many methods of meditation as there are people. The key is discovering which method or combination of methods works best for you. In exploring past lives, certain kinds of meditation lend themselves more easily to accessing this information within the deeper levels of the mind.

When you close your eyes and withdraw your senses from the world around you, you enter another realm of life entirely. It is more fleeting and fluid than the physical world, but it is just as real. It has the power to touch your life and enhance it in ways that we are only now beginning to understand. It is a world where you can dream, ponder the future, unveil the mysteries around you or even rediscover your pasts.

Meditation is not a difficult process. Seeing is the real problem. In learning to shift your awareness, the manner in which you perceive the world, you will use an altered state of consciousness. We have all experienced altered states. Dreaming is but one example. Reading often "takes people out of themselves." Jogging, needlework, long drives and listening to music are all activities that produce shifts in consciousness. Through meditation, we learn to shift our consciousness in a controlled manner.

Most effective meditation techniques, regardless of their purpose, are very simple. They depend upon capacities that anyone with some degree of intelligence can develop with time and practice. With the past life meditation techniques described in this chapter, anyone can achieve some results almost immediately.

A good past life meditation technique is founded upon three basic abilities: visualization, concentration and creative imagination.

Visualization is the ability to create a mental picture and hold it steady within the mind. Such pictures should be made as lifelike as possible. A simple practice exercise is to visualize an orange, clearly seeing its shape, size and color. In your mind, feel the skin of the orange. What does it feel like as you press your fingers into it to peel it? Notice the fragrance as the juice squirts out. Try to create the image of its taste as well.

Concentration is the art of holding the image strongly within your mind without wandering to other things. With practice, we can learn to hold a concentrated focus to the exclusion of others. Try counting slowly to ten. Visualize each number in your mind, and hold that number to the exclusion of any other thought, until the next number is counted.

I often use this exercise in my classes to demonstrate that it is not as easy as it seems. I do not count at a regular speed. If other thoughts arise, more work is needed—even such thoughts as, "Oh, this isn't so difficult." More will be covered on this aspect in the next chapter in the discussion of the phenomenon of "resistance."

The third ability to be developed for good past life meditation is the creative imagination — enabling the mind to create images and scenes associated with the meditative seed thoughts. These images should be created in three-dimensional form. If you have been working with the exercise in the last chapter, you will see this working. The seed thought is that of an art gallery in which an old portrait of you hangs. What appears in that portrait, though, is not given to you. Your own imagination must create that.

Creative imagination, or imaginative cognition, is the key to opening the doors to true spiritual awareness of energies and beings. Energy translated from those more ethereal realms must take the form of images for us to be able to recognize them and work with them. The imagination is a reality in some form on levels beyond our normal, sensory world. Through it, we create a new awareness, a new experience in form and color in relation to this world.

When applied to past life meditations, imagination triggers higher forms of intuition and inspiration. We open to a new understanding of the conditions of our lives. A physically and spiritually creative individual intuitively sees possibilities for transforming ordinary data and experiences into a new creation. It enables us to make new discoveries about ourselves, and it provides illumination that can free us from karmic cycles.

Inside each of our skulls, we have a double brain with two ways of knowing. The different characteristics of the two hemispheres of the brain have a dynamic role in our being able to effectively utilize altered states of consciousness for past life discovery.

Each hemisphere gathers in the same information but handles it differently. One, often the dominant left hemisphere, has a tendency to take over and inhibit the other half, especially among people in the Western world. This left hemisphere analyzes, counts, marks time, plans, views logically and follows step-by-step procedures. It verbalizes, makes statements and draws conclusions based on logic. It is sequential and linear in its approach to life.

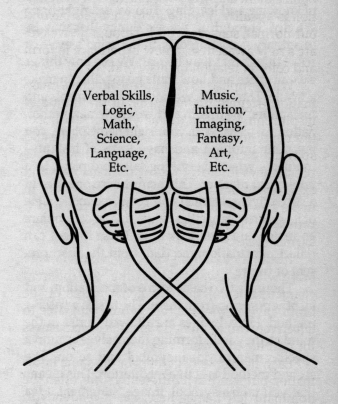

Verbal Skills, Logic, Math, Science, Language, Etc.

Music, Intuition, Imaging, Fantasy, Art, Etc.

THE TWO HEMISPHERES OF THE BRAIN
When we use altered states, such as in past life meditation, it is easier to go through the right hemisphere to those deeper levels of the subconscious mind. Here those ancient memories are still stored for us.

On the other hand, we do have a second way of knowing and learning. This we call right-brain activity. Through it, we see things that may be imaginary—existing only in the mind's eye—or recall things that may be real. We see how things exist in space and how parts go together to make a whole. Through it, we understand symbols and metaphors, we dream and we create new combinations of ideas. With your right hemisphere, you tap your intuition and have leaps of insight—moments when everything falls into place, in a nonlogical manner. This hemisphere operates in a subjective, relational and time-free mode. One of its greatest capacities is imaging. It can conjure an image and then look at it. These images can reflect information and data from the past, present or future.

There are two basic forms of meditation, and all others spring from them. The first is a passive method. Here, images are allowed to rise in the mind as they will, forming themselves around a specific mantra, idea, symbol and so on. The second method is active meditation. This means that you take a symbol, image, statement, idea and so on and mull it over in your mind to the exclusion of all other thoughts. The idea is to extract everything that you can about that idea or symbol. The most effective means of meditation for past life exploration is the active form.

In past life meditation, you use the image-forming capability of your right brain to access

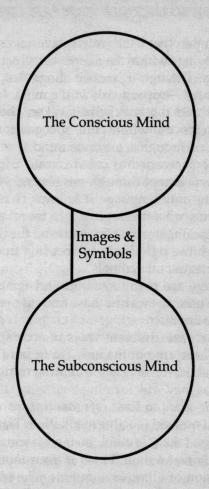

The Conscious Mind

Images &
Symbols

The Subconscious Mind

BRIDGING THE CONSCIOUS AND SUBCONSCIOUS MINDS

Through the right brain's imaging ability, we can bridge to the subconscious mind and awaken our past life memories.

the deeper levels of your subconscious more strongly. It is within the deeper levels of the subconscious that our ancient memories can be uncovered. Proper work with specific kinds of images and symbols helps awaken those past life memories within the subconscious and bridge them to the conscious mind.

The subconscious mind cannot communicate to us except through images and symbols. It is the only language it knows. Thus, if we want to send a message to it to reveal past life information, we must learn to send the message through the right brain by focusing upon specific images and symbols.

There are many symbols and images that can be used to awaken those ancient memories. As you are discovering, each chapter is presenting you with different ways of accomplishing this. These are not the only ways, but they are easy and effective. They will bring results.

Aids to Past Life Meditation

There are many effective ways of facilitating an altered state of consciousness, especially for past life exploration. Three of the most effective are fragrances, flower essences and crystals and stones. They alter the energy of the environment and help establish a mindset appropriate to the purpose of the meditation. They assist us in achieving and maintaining concentration and focus upon our past life images.

Past Life Fragrances

Fragrance—whether used through herbs, oils or incense—is one of the most effective means of inducing an altered state of consciousness. Fragrances alter the vibrational energy of the environment and the individual, each according to its own unique properties. Fragrances affect us on subtle but very real psychological levels. They assist us in more easily penetrating the consciousness on deeper levels.

In past life meditations, fragrances, especially essential oils, assist you in moving from your outer focus to an inner awareness. There are a number of ways in which they can be employed. The oils can be applied to a bath before the meditation. In this way, the fragrance is absorbed into the body and remains throughout the meditation. A half capful per bath is all that is necessary; the essential oils are very potent.

You can also anoint yourself with a drop or two of oil prior to the meditation itself. (You may wish to dilute it with water first, as some oils can be irritating to the skin.) You can also place a drop or two in a small bowl of water and set it near you in the area where you will be performing the past life meditation. The fragrance will fill the air around you.

In the case of incenses, you can burn them before the meditation. If it is a stick incense, you can have it burning throughout the entire meditation.

There are ten fragrances that are very effective in past life meditations. They are not listed in the order of effectiveness; this you must discover for yourself. We each have our own unique energy system, and that system will respond differently from anyone else. Use the list as a guideline. Experiment. Mix and match. Find the fragrance or combination of fragrances that has the strongest effect upon you.

Eucalyptus

This is a powerful and versatile meditation oil. Place a drop between the eyes, and it serves to stimulate inner vision (activation of the third eye). It also helps prevent being negatively affected by any emotions that are aroused through the past life meditation.

Frankincense

This is an excellent all-purpose fragrance for meditation of any kind. It can be used to induce vision. It helps to open you to higher inspiration and clearer perspectives. When used with past life meditations, it can help you to clarify any obsessive behaviors that are a result of the past.

Hyacinth

Hyacinth is an excellent fragrance for anyone who employs the rebirthing process, a regression to the actual trauma of birth. It can be used in past life meditation to reveal the sources of depression. It is effective for pregnant mothers who perform meditations to attune to the soul who is about to enter. (These meditations are discussed further in chapter 6.)

Lavender

Lavender has always been considered a magical herb with a magical fragrance. It can be used to help stimulate dreams of past lives, especially in meditations performed prior to sleep. It can be used effectively to shed light on conflicts with spouses that may have their origins in the past. It is a fragrance that helps to reveal karmic blockages and how best to remove them. It also effective when used with past life meditations designed to reveal the origins of emotional blocks or inner conflicts that are interfering with your spiritual growth.

Lilac

This fragrance is excellent in past life meditations, as it stimulates the deeper levels of conscious memory. It is especially effective if used to anoint the back of the head, at the point of the medulla oblongata. It will spiritualize the meditative experience. It assists in recalling past lives by inducing greater memory and clairvoyance. It stimulates a greater realization of the innate beauty of the soul of the individual.

Myrrh

Myrrh is a powerful fragrance that has been used in the past for healing and cleansing. It can stimulate memories of past lives that are creating blocks within your life. It can also stimulate past life revelations in the dream state.

Orange

Orange fragrance can be used in past life therapy to help release emotional traumas. It brings clarity and calmness to highly charged states. It can also stimulate past life dreams that provide clues to the unknown origin of fears.

Sage

Sage is a powerful fragrance that can open us up to the spiritual impact of the past upon the present. It has a capacity, when used in past life meditation, to reveal all times to us. It also serves to stimulate greater understanding and integration of the past with the present. It awakens a sense of immortality and the realization that the life of the soul extends far beyond one physical incarnation. It helps clarify the spiritual development of the past in relation to the present.

Sandalwood

Sandalwood is a good general, all-purpose fragrance. It eases the individual into a nice altered state. Application to the temples assists in concentration during meditation. It helps to remove blockages that can prevent higher revelations in the meditative state.

Wisteria

Occultists, metaphysicians and healers have used this fragrance in many ways to open to higher vibrations. It can be used in past life med-itations to awaken and activate the creativity that has been developed in the past. It helps open the doors between the conscious mind and the sub-conscious in which our more ancient memories are stored. It stimulates illumination of the past.

Past Life Flower Essences

Flower essences are elixirs made from the flowers of various plants, herbs and trees. They are not made from the physical material of the plant, but rather the energy operating behind and through the plant is extracted through a simple alchemical procedure. They are entirely benign and they do not conflict with any other form of medicine.

Every flower has its own personality and its own vibrational frequency. Each has its own unique effect upon the individual. It is that energy pattern that is infused into the elixir. The liquid, taken in the form of several drops, can then be used to transmute, alter or create new vibrational patterns for the individual. They can be used in achieving very specific functions and purposes. Those listed below are effective when taken in conjunction with any past life explo-ration—meditation or otherwise.

Blackberry

Blackberry is effective with any creative visualization and meditation. It brings clarity for the solving of past problems that are recurring in the present life. It helps to reawaken the higher teachings of the past so they can be re-expressed in the present.

Black-Eyed Susan

This flower essence is dynamic when used with any past life therapy. It helps stimulate penetrating insight into blocked areas of the present that have their origin in the past. It helps open up new perspectives on death and dying. It is useful when there is unconscious resistance to working with key issues of the past.

California Poppy

California poppy helps to stimulate inner vision and intuition. It is an excellent aid to any form of meditation. It can also be effective for those who get caught up in the glamour of who they might have been in the past. It helps release gently the karma of the past that is still held deeply within the heart

Chaparral

Chaparral stimulates deeper states of consciousness. It is effective for seeing the patterns of the present that are new expressions of the patterns of the past. It can be used to help stimulate dreams that reveal information and issues of the past that are still affecting us.

Forget-Me-Not

This essence stimulates deeper levels of memory, and helps awaken communication between the conscious mind and the subconscious. It is especially effective in past life meditations in uncovering karmic connections with the people most important to our life.

Iris

Iris helps unlock the creative aspects we have developed in the past. It enables us to use our past life explorations for greater inspiration and rejuvenation.

Lotus

This essence enhances the effects of any other flower essence. It awakens the deeper levels of consciousness. It can be used in the post-meditation process to synthesize and integrate the past life experience with our present circumstances. It is a dynamic aid to any form of meditation.

Mugwort

Mugwort increases our awareness during meditations. It stimulates the intuition and the creative imagination. It can also be used to stimulate dreams of the past. It opens insight into the present based upon the meditative experience.

Saint John's Wort

This is one of the most beneficial essences for any mediative practice. It eases one gently into an altered state. It is also very dynamic in stimulating dreams of past lives. It eases any fears an individual may have about opening the doors to the past. It strengthens our perceptions in the meditative state, and it can awaken new perspectives and attitudes on death and dying.

Self-Heal

Self-heal helps us face up to the task of our karma—be it from the past or part of the present. In past life meditations, it helps reveal the learning of the past which is being expanded in the present. It helps an individual to release the past so that progress can be made in the present. It can show us through the meditation what has carried over into the present from the past that still needs to be healed.

Star Tulip

Star tulip is an excellent remedy for greater past life recall. It can help you remember those dreams that have revealed aspects of your past lives. It awakens greater intuitive sensitivity, enhancing any meditative experience. It can assist us in harmonizing the past with the present more effectively.

Thyme

Thyme helps ease us gently into altered states of consciousness. It increases our intuitive perceptions, and it is excellent for time recall and all past life therapies.

Past Life Crystals and Stones

Crystals, stones and gems have had great popularity in the past decade, but their uses extend into the ancient past. They are natural forms of electrical energy, known as piezoelectrical energy. Each stone or crystal releases its own frequency, and thus some are very effective for helping to induce specific kinds of altered states.

Simply holding the appropriate crystal or stone in your hand during the past life meditation will cause it to work. In some cases you may wish to tape a small piece to the forehead in the area between your eyes. This will help to set the electrical energy into motion so that it stimulates the third eye, your inner vision.

Although any quartz crystal can be programmed to assist in awakening past life information, some crystals and stones do this more naturally:

Amethyst

This is an excellent stone for any meditation process. It helps transmute normal consciousness into the deeper levels of the subconscious mind. Its violet color is a combination of red and blue—the physical and the spiritual, the present and the past.

Carnelian

This orange stone takes its name from a Latin word which means "flesh." It has ties to the "flesh" of our past and the "flesh" of our present. In past life meditation, it can bring insight into how to use the past life knowledge to reshape the present.

Double-Terminated Clear Quartz

A double-terminated quartz has a point on both ends. This is a very effective meditation tool, regardless of the kind of meditation. It is symbolic—with its two points—of the connection of one level with another. In past life exploration, it helps stimulate awareness of how the past is reflecting itself within the present.

Hematite

This gray, silver stone is effective for awakening the subconscious mind and its memory banks. It is especially effective in past life regressions through hypnosis. It opens the past life awareness gently and assists the individual into putting it into present perspective.

Lapis Lazuli

This stone is powerful in past life therapy, especially if a piece is taped to the forehead during the meditation. It awakens inner vision that can enable us to penetrate into areas of the subconscious that may be blocked or which we may resist. It can help stimulate awareness of the past that needs to be cleansed, that is no longer necessary to carry around with us. It helps to identify, release and heal old patterns and wounds that we have carried over into our present life.

Phantom Crystals

These are very powerful to use in past life meditations. They hint of realms and dimensions of true reality. Those which contain earth elements within them that form the phantom (such as with lead) are even more effective. They symbolize the life of the past that is a phantom that follows us in the present.

Tabular Crystals

Tabular crystals are also effective to use in past life meditations. Tabulars are flat quartz crystals, with two opposite sides being larger and much wider. They are a link between the past and the present, the conscious and the subconscious, the physical and the spiritual. They stimulate an awareness of how to link two points. In past life meditations, they serve to help us integrate the lessons of the past with the present in a positive manner, so that we do not repeat the old patterns. They also balance any strong emotional responses to past life revelations.

6

Past Life Therapy Through the Tree of Life

There are many images that are effective in meditation for stimulating past life memory. Whatever scenario that you choose to use, choose it consciously. Make sure that the images reflect your purpose. Learning to employ and focus specific images for specific effects is a magical process. If you are performing a past life meditation, make sure that the images encompassing the framework of the meditation are appropriate to it. If they are not, your subconscious memory will be difficult to access.

It is also important to understand that the soul creates safeguards for us. Unless you are abusing past life exploration (doing it every night, getting caught up in the glamour, never looking for practical applications, and so on), the information you receive will always be centered only around past lives that are affecting you now. The difficulty, though, often arises in understanding *where* and *how* that past life is affecting you now.

There are ways of working with past life exploration, though, that can help reveal to you what areas of your life are most being affected. You can explore past lives in a very directed manner. For example, if you are having romantic problems, there is a way of performing a past life meditation that will show you whether the problems encountered are the effect of a past life or whether they represent a new learning experience in the present.

You can accomplish this with a form of Qabalistic meditation. The Qabala is an ancient form of mysticism that on one level teaches how the universe was formed, and on a more practical level teaches how to access the different levels of the conscious mind so that we can tap the varied energies of the universe. It teaches us how to go within ourselves to those levels of the subconscious mind through which we can gain access to the different forces and energies of heavens.

The Tree of Life is the primary image for teaching this process. It is a diagram depicting ten levels. Each level represents a specific level of the subconscious mind. Each level also has a series of corresponding energies and characteristics associated with it, and we have access to them if we learn to open that level of the subconscious. This book does not intend to teach all

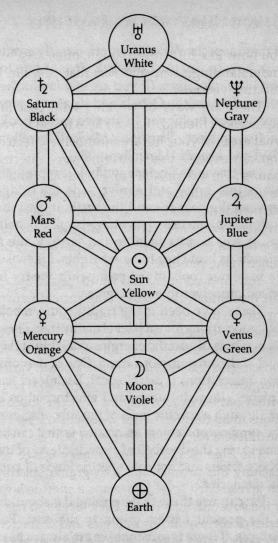

THE TREE OF LIFE

of these aspects. We will concern ourselves only with how to use the Qabalistic Tree of Life for past life exploration. (If you are seeking further information on the Qabala and its many correspondences, I refer you to my two earlier books on that subject: *Simplified Magic* [Llewellyn, 1989] and *Imagick* [Llewellyn, 1989].)

The tree is an ancient symbol. It represents things that grow and evolve. It is the bridge between the heavens and the earth. In past life exploration, the use of its image is quite beneficial. A tree has its roots in the earth, while it extends its branches to new heights. Likewise, we have our roots in the past, while we try to extend ourselves to new heights.

There have been many traditional symbols and associations for each level on the tree. These are symbols of specific energies available at that level of the subconscious mind. One of the common associations is astrological. Each level has a planet whose influence and effect upon us is felt through a specific level of the subconscious. The symbols and colors associated with it can be used to ring the doorbell of a specific level of the subconscious and activate specific kinds of past life memories.

We can use these to determine if a situation in the present has its origin in the past. For example, if there is someone we are always having conflicts with, we can use the symbols and images associated with the "Mars Level" to reveal whether this is a conflict that originated in the past or something new that we must learn to handle. To do this, we will simply adapt the meditation we learned in the previous chapter to the Tree of Life technique.

To understand how this works, we must first understand what kinds of information are available to us at each level of the Tree of Life. These levels of the subconscious can be used to explore any issue, relationship or ability—positive or negative—that may have had its origin or pattern established in a past life.

Keep in mind, though, that, even if you discover an ability in the past, it does not mean that it is fully functional in the present. That which we have developed in the past must be reawakened, redeveloped and taken to yet further heights (be it an ability or a relationship).

Yes, if you have developed something in the past, it may be a little easier to bring it back to where it was than it would be to unfold it for the first time, but effort and time are still required. We can compare this to learning to read. Some individuals find it easier than others, but all have to go through the same basics and step-by-step process. Regardless of the past, the individual must still rewin the conditions for higher illumination. Discovering what we have developed in the past, though, can provide guidance for our present lines of development.

Earth Level

This is where we are in the present. This is where we always start in our meditation. You want to relate and apply everything to yourself in the present. Remember: if what you experience does not help you solve a problem, help you put a situation into a new perspective, help you to handle something more productively or provide new understanding, then it is not serving any purpose.

Moon Level

Activating this level of the subconscious mind and performing the past life meditation can show you why things happen when they do. It can be used to help you find past life origins—if any—for major delays within your life plans. This level can open past life information about any of your emotions—good, bad or indifferent. It can also be used to show you the circumstances in which you opened up your intuition in the past.

Mercury Level

If you activate this level of the subconscious and perform past life meditation, it can reveal connections to *education*, such as links between you and your teacher(s) or between you and your student(s). Any issues involving education, truth, communication and the sciences can be illuminated through this level of the subconscious. If someone in your life has difficulty being truthful to you, this is the level that can reveal any past life relations to this issue. If you have difficulty with the truth yourself, this is again the level. Difficulty speaking or hearing when others speak may be explained through past life exploration at this level.

Venus Level

This is the level of the subconscious you should activate if you wish to reveal past life patterns and connections in your relationships, especially the romantic ones. Issues concerning sexuality and relating to others may reveal their origins in past lives more easily through this particular level. This is the level to use to discover past life sources for the development of creative and artistic energies and abilities. In cases of child prodigies, this level can help you discover the past life experiences which helped manifest this way in the present.

Sun Level

This is the level to activate in past life exploration for anything dealing with health and personal well-being. Issues surrounding religion may originate in the past and can more easily be revealed through this level of the subconscious. This level can reveal whether insecurity, jealousy or pride originated in past lives. Idealism, strong compassion and the ability to heal, on the other hand, are often the result of past life endeavors. Again, this level can provide illumination on that development.

Mars (and Pluto) Level

Performing a past life exploration at this level of the subconscious can reveal past life links to destructive issues and relationships. Cruelty and strength of will (battles of will) can have origins in past lives, as can critical judgment and a strong sense of discrimination. Protectiveness of those around you may have its source in the past as well. This level can provide insight into the origins of enemies within your life, discord and what you have chosen to overcome in the present life. This is the level to use to discover if hyperactivity and other imbalanced energy expressions will reveal their origins in past lives. Use this level to discover how you have slain your dragons in the past. Lessons in transitions, the tearing down of the old and so on may have their origins in the past as well.

Jupiter Level

This is the level of the subconscious mind that we should activate to discover past life sources for issues of abundance and money. This level can provide understanding of the justice (or lack of it) within your life. It can be used to reveal the paths you have taken in your past spiritual quests. This is a level that can reveal the higher aspects of mercy and peace that you have developed in the past and how they are affecting you in the present. Problems with hypocrisy, dogmatism, smugness and self-righteousness can also have their origins in the past. Past life meditation at this level will reveal if this is so. It can also reveal the origins of our sense of commitment and idealism.

Saturn Level

Activating this level of the subconscious and performing the past life meditation will help you in seeing those sorrows, burdens and sacrifices which you have brought with you from the past. You should connect with this level to understand your relationship with your mother, or a relationship of parent to child in the past. If you are a mother or father to be, it is the level that can reveal your past life connection to the incoming soul. Past life family connections and relationships can be revealed here in general. If it is a particular issue, such as always fighting with a brother or sister, you may wish to explore the past life associations through the Mars Level.

In Qabalistic teachings, this is the level through which you can open access to the true Akashic records, the recordings of all that you have ever done on any level at any time. Individuals who may be deaf and/or dumb can find the past life connection—if any—through this level of the subconscious. This is the level to use to understand past life sources of fears—known and unknown. It is also a level at which you can learn how you have developed higher forms of intuition in the past. This is the level to use to discover lessons associated with birth and death that have been brought over from the past.

Neptune Level

This is a level of the subconscious that you can use to understand your past ties to your father. Fathers can use this effectively to unfold ties to their children. This level can reveal past life abilities that have been hidden from you and which you can reawaken in your present life. Any new endeavor that has a source in a past life can be revealed through this level. Superstition, fear of the future or being "spaced out" may also have its source in the past; the Neptune Level can reveal it. Any past lives and existences that have occurred on other planets may reveal themselves here. Interests in astronomy and astrology may have their origins in the past as well. If so, this level of the subconscious will reveal it.

Uranus Level

This is a level of the subconscious that we can use to reveal past life sources of creativity that we can easily reawaken. It is a level at which we can open ourselves to information about our personal spiritual issues. Feelings of being misunderstood or never feeling as if we belong anywhere can have past life sources which can be uncovered through this level of the subconscious. If issues of self-denial, very deep negative self-images and problems with facing reality have their origins in the past, this is a level that can reveal them. There are ways of using this level of the subconscious to open vision to the next birth—for revelations of future life progressions.

EXERCISE:
USING THE TREE OF LIFE IN
PAST LIFE MEDITATIONS

Activating one of these levels of your sub-conscious is not difficult. The color associated with it and its astrological symbol are all that is necessary. The symbol and the color are incorporated into the meditation, but you can create a proper mindset by simply burning a candle that is the color associated with the level.

Color affects us on physical, emotional, mental and spiritual levels. It triggers specific kinds of responses within the mind. If you want to stimulate the *Sun Level*, light a yellow candle. As the candle burns throughout the meditation, its energy will interact with your aura, surrounding you, penetrating you and stimulating the appropriate level of your subconscious. This, when combined with the images in an appropriate past life scenario, will help release past life information along the desired lines.

Meditation with any of the levels of the Tree of Life works much better once you have achieved some success with opening the "Gallery of Your Life" (chapter 4). It is much easier to explore specific issues and lifetimes once you have opened up access to the past in general.

Use the "Gallery of Life " exercise as a warmup. Perform it the day before you begin working with the Tree of Life. Then perform the Tree of Life exercise for three days in a row.

Three establishes a creative rhythm and helps to activate the past life information more creatively and powerfully. If the effects are minimal, wait a week and then repeat this procedure. Rarely will you have to repeat more than twice to achieve the desired results.

1. Decide what issue you wish to explore from a past life level. For example, you may wish to understand something about your mother.

2. Then decide which level is most appropriate for that issue. Since mother information is most appropriate to the *Saturn Level*, that is the level of the subconscious you will want to activate and use with your past life meditation.

3. Make preparations, just as you did with the meditation at the end of the last chapter. Take the phone off the hook. Make sure no one will disturb you.

4. Gather your past life meditation aids; i.e., fragrance, flower essence and/or crystal. Have the appropriate candle ready as well. Review the symbol for the level you will be accessing.

5. Now light the candle and the incense. Close your eyes and begin several minutes of rhythmic breathing as explained earlier. Then move on to a progressive relaxation, focusing on each part of your body, sending warm and soothing energies to each in turn.

6. Now visualize within your mind's eye the scene that follows:

You are in a beautiful meadow. It is fresh and green. Wildflowers are everywhere. In the middle of this meadow is a giant oak tree. It is ancient and gnarled, and its massive branches extend upward past the clouds and into the heavens themselves. You can see that its roots must extend deep into the very heart of the earth.

You step closer, and you notice that there is a small door etched into the tree at its base. As you step even closer, you are amazed. Carved into the bark of the door is the symbol for Earth, a circle with an equal-armed cross within it. Below that insignia, you see your full name at birth carved intricately into the bark as well. You understand instinctively that this is *your* Tree of Life that contains the roots of your past and the buds of your future.

The door swings open, inviting you in. As you step through, you find yourself in a softly lit chamber. It is warm and peaceful. The floor and the walls are splashed with the colors of the earth—browns, greens, russets and golds. You step in further, and at the back of the chamber you see a golden staircase that descends down through a mist far below.

7. At this point you follow the stairs down just as you did in the meditation at the end of chapter 4. At the bottom, you find yourself in a

circular room. At the end of the room is that same massive door, but it is painted the color of the level of your subconscious that you have chosen to activate. (If it is the Saturn Level, then the door will be black. If you are on the Jupiter level, the door will be blue.)

Your name is carved into the door just as before, but so is the symbol (the astrological glyph) of the level you have chosen. The door opens, spilling out gold and blue light that blesses, heals and draws you in. As you step across the threshold, the door closes, the blue and gold light dissipates and you find yourself in that ancient gallery, but now it is the color of the level you are activating. All of the artifacts, remnants, sculptures, walls, floor and ceiling are in that color. (If it is the Saturn level, then everything is black. If it is the Jupiter level, then the entire gallery is blue.)

8. You move to the wall upon which the original portrait hung. As you do, you see that there are now *two* life-size portrait frames. In the center of each portrait canvas is a large astrological symbol for that level, in the color for that level. If it is the Saturn level, you will visualize a large astrological glyph for Saturn (♄) in the color black in the center of the canvas. Encircling the portrait frames are rings of astrological glyphs for that level.

As you focus on the right-hand portrait, the astrological symbol fades, and there now forms a present-day image of you and the person to whom you wish to uncover your past connection. If it is not a person but rather an issue, visualize a scene within the right-hand portrait that depicts the issue in some way.

Now turn your focus to the left-hand portrait. Allow the image of the astrological symbol within the center of it to fade. As it does, allow a new scene to appear. At this point follow the same procedure you used in the previous meditation.

Remember that this is your gallery. Look for the brass plates. Feel the engravings. Allow the image to crystallize. Ask yourself questions. What is the relationship? What kind of life was it? Trust your impressions. Allow the scene to change and reveal other aspects of that lifetime if it chooses to do so. What emotions are being experienced. What is occurring? As the images reveal themselves to you, occasionally glance back at the right-hand portrait to see how those events of the past are affecting you in the present.

Allow the word or phrase which was the gift of that lifetime to reveal itself at the top of the portrait.

9. At this point, you allow the image on the left to fade and be replaced by the astrological symbol. Then you allow the image in the right-hand portrait to fade and also be replaced by the

astrological symbol. Step back from the portraits and move to the door. See yourself being surrounded by the blue and gold light, and, as the door to exit the gallery opens, step out.

10. At this point you ascend the stairs just as in the original meditation. When you reach the top of the stairs, you are standing in that earth-colored room inside the Tree of Life. You step across the floor and outside the Tree itself. As the door closes behind you, you see the engraving of the Earth symbol and your own name upon it. Now allow the image of the meadow to dissipate and allow your awareness of your present state to return with peace and comfort.

Record your experience within the Gallery. By recording these exercises in your Past Life Journal, you will find that the scenes will clarify themselves and even more information and insight will come through.

If no image appeared in the portrait on the left, wait a day and then perform the exercise again. Repeat this a third time if necessary. If nothing appears after the third time, the current connection is probably a new learning situation arising for the first time in this incarnation. If the experience was not as dynamic as you hoped but you did experience something, wait a day or two and then repeat it again. You will find that it will improve each time.

Don't lock yourself too rigidly into this format. Once you have the basic meditation procedure down, adapt it. Experiment with it. Remember, though, that the key to unlocking memories in regard to specific issues lies in utilizing the color and the symbols. As you learn to do this, you will find that there is very little that you cannot discover about yourself.

7

Self Hypnosis and Past Life Awareness

Hypnosis is one of the most common ways of exploring past lives. However, in recent times it has fallen under suspicion. Some suggest that hypnosis is not a viable tool in that the hypnotist makes suggestions as to what the client should or should not experience. Although this may be true in some cases, a good past life hypnotist will simply provide the skeletal framework that will facilitate a past life memory for the client. Again, the key is to remember that what is important is whether the past life information can be used productively, regardless of how it is obtained.

The A.M.A once defined hypnosis as an increase in suggestibility. It is a means of activating the subconscious mind for a particular function. The conscious mind is the seat of our organized brain activity and our will power. It is what we use when active, awake and aware, but it only controls about 10 per cent of the body and brain. The subconscious mind, on the other hand, is the seat of our memory bank, our self-image, our perceptions of others and our intuition. It controls about 90 per cent of the body and brain functions, including the autonomic nervous system. Through hypnosis we can more effectively access these different functions.

Before 1950 the primary applications of hypnosis were healing and entertainment. Today there are many other therapeutic and nontherapeutic applications, including everything from weight control to stress release to self-confidence and even past life discovery.

Hypnosis does not mean "put to sleep" or being unaware of your surroundings. You do not have to achieve a deep stage in order to be helped or to experience the effects. In fact, 95 per cent of the adult population is capable of achieving a light trance state, and that is all that is necessary for the subconscious to be activated and for the session to be effective.

There are other misconceptions about hypnosis as well. You cannot be made to do anything against your morals. You will often be completely aware of your surroundings. It does not require a weak mind to be effective. You cannot be made to divulge your secrets, and it is not antireligious.

These statements are, of course, generalizations. Yes, there are subtle ways of using hyp-

	SYMPTOMS
	Rapport
	Relaxation
	Closing of Eyes
	Complete Physical
	Relaxation
HYPNOIDAL AND	Fluttering of Eyelids
LIGHT/MEDIUM TRANCE	Eye Catalepsy
CONDITIONS ARE	Limb Catalepsy
RECOGNIZABLE	Analgesia
	Complete Physical
	and Mental Relaxation
	Anesthesia
	Partial Amnesia
	Post-Hypnotic Suggestion
	Response

RECOGNIZING HYPNOTIC EFFECTS

Ninety-Five percent of the adult population is capable of achieving a light to medium trance condition on the first attempt. This is all that is necessary in order to access the subconscious mind and achieve results through a past life regression. The symptoms are some tangible clues that let the hypnotist know that the light trance condition has been achieved and that the past life exploration can then proceed.

nosis to stimulate the subconscious through backdoor avenues that can circumvent moral dispositions and even help unlock secrets. It takes someone very skilled in hypnosis and very well trained in clinical therapy to do so effectively. The hypnotic techniques given in this text for past life exploration are straightforward and will not involve such processes.

Hypnosis is a naturally induced, profound state of relaxation. It requires some intelligence, a willingness to achieve the altered state, concentration and proper motivation. It enables you to bypass the conscious mind to access the subconscious.

Before we can use it to our full benefit, especially in past life exploration, there must be a better understanding of the principles involved, especially those which can help identify and influence our growth and behavior patterns. The usual—force, drugs, reward, punishment and reasoning—are not nearly so effective as suggested images that are introduced while we are in an altered state of consciousness.

We will be using a four-step hypnotic procedure in past life exploration. At the end of this chapter is a word-by-word hypnotic induction that you can use yourself. It employs all four steps.

1. Induce the Altered State of Consciousness

If you have been performing the previous exercises in this book, you will already have this aspect down pat. It is the focus upon the deep, rhythmic breathing.

2. Deepen the Altered State of Consciousness

For this part we will also use what we have already learned—the progressive relaxation. We will focus our attention upon and relax each part of the body in turn. Take your time with this part. The deeper the relaxation, the greater the effects of the entire session.

3. Maintain and Use the Altered State

In this stage we will employ specific imagery and suggestions to stimulate the subconscious to reveal specific past life memories.

4. Termination and Emergence

This stage involves the use of positive reinforcement regarding the experience and the gentle return to the normal state of consciousness. It is a good point at which to use post-hypnotic suggestions for future explorations and positive acceptance and use of the experience.

How Hypnotic Suggestion and Images Work

Our subconscious responds to suggestions and images in a very definable manner. There is an old occult axiom which states, "*All* energy follows thought." Where we put our thoughts, that is where our energy goes. We must keep in mind that the subconscious reacts and responds in a very literal manner to our thoughts and words.

We tell our friends that we have "lost" 10 pounds, and the subconscious is activated. "Lost?" it says. "I'd better go find it." And then it starts working with your body and mind functions so that the 10 pounds are recovered. (It usually throws in a few extra just in case you "lose" them again.) We tell ourselves that we catch two colds every winter, and the subconscious starts working with your physiological system so that, as winter comes on, you are more susceptible to "catching" those two colds. For this reason hypnotic suggestions and images should always be clear, pleasant and positively stated.

In hypnosis, there are four primary Laws of Suggestion and Imaging.

1. Law of Concentrated Attention

Whenever you concentrate your attention on an idea over and over again, the idea tends to realize itself. The more you concentrate upon it in an altered state of consciousness, the faster and stronger will be that realization.

2. Law of Reverse Effect

The harder you try to do something, the less likely it is that you will succeed. This is because, if you are trying too hard, you are not relaxing enough to allow the powerful subconscious to do the work for you. Your tense and anxious effort sends an unspoken message to the subconscious that there is fear of failure, which then tends to realize itself.

3. Law of Dominant Effect

A strong emotion will replace a weaker one. Let the stronger emotion surface. It is a cleansing and healing process. A common example is seen when anger explodes and then is replaced by calm. Through self-hypnosis, we can release the strong emotions of past lives that are still affecting us in a controlled manner. Implied also within this law, in regard to past life regressions, is the idea that those past lives that are most strongly and emotionally affecting you in the present are the ones that will be uncovered first.

4. Law of Will Power and Imagination

Anytime will power challenges the imagination, the imagination will win. Will power is part of the conscious mind, and imagination is part of the subconscious mind's activities. The subconscious mind is stronger. We cannot just consciously will ourselves to remember past lives. We use the imagination, through suggestions, to stimulate the subconscious to release the energy and/or information required.

There is a phenomena that is encountered in hypnosis and in meditation. It is called *resistance*. Resistance occurs on the subconscious level of the mind. It is that point in the session where the mind wanders or argues with the suggestion or "raises its eyebrows" at the images being used.

This is actually a positive signal. It tells you you have touched the subconscious!

Through controlled altered states such as meditation and hypnosis, we work to control and direct the subconscious mind. After years of being allowed to run around and do whatever it wants, when it wants, it resists being controlled. It tries to avoid following the suggestion or image. Thus it seeks to distract the mind and stay unfocused.

When you notice the mind wandering, do not get upset. Upset will only bring you back to a conscious state of mind. Simply bring your attention back to the point of focus. You may have to repeat this a number of times, but each time you return to your focus, you are teaching the subconscious to follow you rather than the other way around. And your sessions will be increasingly effective.

Past Life Awareness Through Self-Hypnosis

Because hypnotic suggestion is so effective, we will use a form of self-hypnosis until you can seek out a qualified, trained hypnotist. Any altered state will increase your susceptibility to suggestion. With self-hypnosis, you are assured of being influenced only by your own thoughts, intonations and directions. I recommend that you tape-record the regression at the end of this chapter, or create your own version of it. Then simply sit or lie down and allow your own voice to lead you into the past life regression.

Certain effects can and will be experienced in any good hypnotic session. Distortion of time is the most common. The individual often feels the time involved has been much greater than it actually was. There can be involuntary bodily movements. These are often twitches as the body begins to relax. The individual may experience specific images and colors, while some may only get an impression. Others may only hear. As mentioned earlier, one is neither better nor worse. It is simply unique to you. There will be an extreme sense of relaxation, heaviness or even lightness that occurs with the relaxation. Sensations of falling asleep, growing, shrinking or even pulling and stretching can occur.

In past life regressions, even when used with self-hypnosis, different people will respond and react differently. You may relive the feelings and the emotions of the past life experience in their full intensity. (In the self-hypnotic induction at the end of this chapter, suggestions are incorporated to soften this effect.) You may see the past life as if you were watching a movie. You may simply have a feeling about a particular time and place, although you may not see or experience anything specific.

A good past life regression helps the individual relive the experience and not just remember it. In the method we will be using, we will be focusing upon just remembering. Keep in mind that past life awareness can open you to emotional and physical pain. It is a catalyst for what ultimately must be dealt with by you. You must find a way to harmonize and integrate it into your present life experience.

Past life hypnosis is not a game, and there are always free variables involved in it. Don't go into it with preconceived notions. Be prepared for the worst-case scenario. Be prepared to face a trauma of the past. This may not ever be revealed, but there is that possibility. Past life regressions can reveal truths about yourself that you may have difficulty accepting and handling.

Above all approach the experience with a healthy sense of discrimination. Weed out uncontrolled fancy and wishful thinking in the past life discovery process. Past life scenarios can be constructed with great intricacy—even if they are only fabrications. Constantly ask yourself: how does this apply to my present? What benefit does this information have for me now? What can this information help me with in my present life? Using your Past Life Journal to record the experience and evaluate it will help you be pragmatic.

Practical Hints in Past Life Self-Hypnosis

The key to a good self-hypnosis session is the induction. The easiest manner of performing this is to tape-record it and then simply play back the recording for yourself. There are key words and phrases that you can incorporate in your induction process to assist you in achieving a deep altered state. Some of these are employed in the sample induction at the end of this chapter, but don't be afraid to be creative. Use this list to make your own phrases:

— sinking down
— going deeper and deeper
— let go
— the deeper you go, the better you feel
— let your body float
— tranquil
— peace . . . peaceful . . . calm
— serene
— pleasing . . . pleasant . . . delightful
— quietness . . . restful
— unwinding
— loosening up . . . flaccid . . . limp
— resting quietly . . . motionless
— heavy . . . heaviness
— good . . . natural . . . smooth
— soothing . . . listless . . . numb
— you have a feeling of well being

Make sure that you are comfortable and will be undisturbed. Remove your glasses (if any) and especially remove the phone from the hook. When recording the induction, use a soft, monotone voice. Repeatedly emphasize the key words ("heavy," "relaxed," "soothing," "quiet," "deeper," and so on). Use short, simple suggestions.

If there is a possibility of outside noises reaching you during the session, use this possibility in the induction to deepen the altered state. For example, include a phrase such as, "Any outside noises will seem very distant and will only serve to relax you more deeply."

We will use a variation of the earlier meditation and simply adapt it to a self-hypnotic session. You may record the session exactly as it appears within this text or adjust it to the manner that you believe will work best for you. Read through it several times before recording it for yourself.

The session is broken down into four distinct levels—the Induction, the Deepening, the Maintaining and Using and the Termination and Emergence. Because a hypnotic session can be very long, you may wish to record the basic induction and the deepening on one side of the tape and the maintaining and the terminations sections on the opposite side. Find what speed and rhythm works for you.

Take your time recording. Most people initially speak too quickly, or they do not allow enough pauses within the session to experience it fully. Some guidelines for these are given within the text, so, as you record the session, you may wish to have a watch or clock nearby. Above all else, have fun with this!

Recording this and playing it at night while

going to sleep will enhance all other past life work you may be involved in. It can be used by itself during the day, and then at night while you go to sleep. One week of this will elicit some dynamic results. This kind of use develops flexibility in the mind and makes all of the past life work discussed in this book more effective.

One possible way of using it is as an amplifier to the Tree of Life exercises:

1. Perform the "Gallery of Life" exercise as a prelude and warmup to the "Tree of Life" work.

2. At night, while you go to sleep, play the recorded regression. Don't worry if you fall asleep. You are simply using this regression to enhance the explorations you pursue while awake.

3. Then, on the following three days, perform the "Tree of Life" past life exploration as already explained.

4. Each of the three nights, use the recorded regression to amplify the effects.

5. Pay close attention to your dreams during these times, especially the emotions generated within the dream scenarios. They will reveal much about the specific avenue you are exploring through the Tree of Life.

(This exercise, like all of the others, can be used either alone or in conjunction with the others. With practice you will find a combination that is effective for you.)

Part One—Basic Induction

"Get yourself into a comfortable position . . . Place your feet on the floor and your hands on your thighs (*For your personal session, you may wish to provide instructions for reclining rather than sitting.*) . . . Now let yourself relax . . . Let your eyes be closed, for this will help you avoid any outside distractions . . . Now relax . . . Think of the word *relaxation* as you have never thought of it before . . . Because now you are going to afford yourself a very peaceful kind of relaxation . . . It is a relaxation that will take over your whole body from the tip of your toes to the top of your head . . . It is a relaxation that will soothe you and open you to the wonders of yourself . . . So let yourself relax now . . . Completely and fully relaxed . . . In a moment I will ask you to concentrate upon your breathing . . . Just simply breathe in . . . and out . . . breathe in . . . and breathe out . . . breathe in relaxation . . . and breathe out tension . . . breathe in . . . and breathe out . . . and let all of the muscles of your face go limp and completely loose . . . breathe in . . . and breathe out . . . feel the shoulder muscles beginning to unwind and relax . . . breathe in . . . and breathe out . . . as you feel the relaxation spreading down your neck and across your shoulders . . . breathe in . . . and breathe out . . . as you feel the relaxation penetrating your arm muscles making them feel so loose and natural . . . breathe in . . . and breathe out . . . breathe in . . . breathe out . . . as all of the muscles of your back begin to loosen up and feel good . . . so good . . . so comfortable . . . so loose . . . breathe in . . . breathe out . . . and allow your chest muscles to relax . . . It feels so good to breathe . . . so effortless . . . so relaxing . . . breathe in . . . breathe out . . . and feel the relaxation penetrating and spreading throughout the muscles of your stomach and thighs . . . breathe in and breathe out . . . as you allow this relaxation to spread through your calf muscles and down to your weary feet . . . breathe in . . . and breathe out . . . as every muscle and fiber in your body feels so good and so comfortable and so relaxed . . . your entire nervous system is sending soothing sensations to each and every part of your body . . . continue to breathe normally . . . relaxing deeply and soundly."

(Pause here for 30 seconds to one minute and then go directly into the Deepening script.)

Part Two—The Deepening

"Now I am going to count from ten to one so that by the time I reach number one you will be completely relaxed . . . so very comfortable . . . in each and every way . . . We'll begin now . . . 10 . . . You are sitting comfortably in your chair, doing nothing but resting . . . You will hear my voice speaking to you all the time, but it will not disturb you . . . You will find as you sit there that your mind is becoming drowsier and drowsier . . . You will try not to think about what I am saying to you, but you will hear everything I say . . . Any noises which occur will seem a long way off and will be of no interest to you . . . Focus on your feet now . . . Let them relax . . . Feel a warm, soothing sensation melting through them and spreading up to your ankles . . . This sensation is warm and relaxing . . . and it begins to soothe and melt past the ankles into the calves . . . It moves slowly and comfortably past the knees and into your thighs . . . as every muscle and nerve feels so limp and loose . . . 9 . . . As I talk to you, you will find that the heavy feeling in your legs increases and, with each breath you take, you feel yourself slowly sinking down . . . You are becoming drowsier and drowsier . . . One part of your mind is already asleep and yet you continue to hear everything I say . . . It feels so good to relax . . . 8 . . . You feel so much better now as your pelvic muscles begin to respond to that warm, soothing sensation . . . You feel it penetrating to your inner organs with a soothing warmth, and it feels so good . . . so very comfortable . . . It's such a wonderful feeling . . . 7 . . . The relaxation is now spreading through your chest muscles . . . Every nerve and fiber begins to relax even more deeply . . . Your breathing is so soothing . . . so effortless . . . and it feels so good . . . 6 . . . Your mental condition is one of quiet rest . . . All you want to do is sink down and down and grow drowsier and drowsier . . . You are resting quietly and peacefully . . . Nothing can worry you and nothing will disturb you . . . You are relaxed . . . 5 . . . Beginning with your lower back muscles, direct that warm soothing sensation into the lower vertebrae . . . Feel it soothing and relaxing . . . spreading upward one by one toward your neck . . . You feel so limp . . . so loose . . . so comfortable . . . Your whole torso feels so good . . . so very good . . . and any outside noises only serve to relax you even more deeply . . . 4 . . . Now your fingertips are responding to your command to relax . . . Feel those soothing sensations spreading towards your wrist . . . forearms . . . the upper arms . . . It feels so good . . . 3 . . . You are not interested in anything except relaxation and what it can do for you . . . You are getting drowsier and drowsier . . . sinking down and down . . . Your neck feels so limp and so loose . . . as every muscle, nerve and fiber is so very relaxed . . . so very comfortable . . . 2 . . . This relaxation is now spreading into your jaw . . . making it limp, loose and comfortable . . . All of your facial muscles feel so very relaxed now . . . Your eyelids feel so comfortable . . . so very comfortable . . . 1 . . . Your scalp feels so very good now . . . Feel all the remaining tension drain right out the top

of your head ... All the tensions and all the cares
... all the worries of the day can be put aside
now and just simply forgotten ... You are beginning to learn how to let go completely ... to sink
down into a deep ... deep ... state of relaxation
... You are feeling so very comfortable ... feeling too tired to care about anything except what
you can attain through relaxation ... You feel
yourself sinking down ... further ... further ...
into a deep ... sound ... state of relaxation ... "

*(Pause here for about 20 to 30 seconds and then
move on to the script for Part Three. Depending on
how long you took for this part, the remainder of the
sellf-hypnotic script might fit more effectively on the
other side of the tape. Pausing to turn the tape over
may briefly interrupt the relaxed state, but not
enough to hinder the entire process.)*

Part Three—Maintaining and Using

"And now I am going to talk to you ... and
as I talk to you, you will relax even more deeply
... I will be asking you to imagine certain scenes
... This imagining will relax you more deeply
... It will make you feel so very good in each
and every way ... You will find that you become
drowsier and drowsier ... relaxing deeper and
deeper ... You will be able to observe them in
an unemotional and detached manner ... They
will relax you, even as you experience them ...

"Imagine yourself at the top of a tall golden
staircase ... Your hand is upon the rail, and you

are prepared to descend . . . You know that, as you descend, you will relax even more deeply than you are now . . . Now I am going to count from five to one and, as I do, you will begin to descend the stairs . . . You will relax even more deeply, and you will be able to step outside of yourself to see new aspects of yourself . . . We'll begin . . . 5 . . . You begin to lightly step down the stairs . . . Each steps relaxes you deeper and deeper . . . As you gently descend, you are amazed at how wonderful it feels to be so relaxed . . . 4 . . . You seem to grow lighter with each step down . . . It almost feels as if you are stepping on soft clouds that gently lower you . . . You have grown so relaxed and so light that your feet barely touch the stairs themselves . . . as you go down . . . down . . . down . . . 3 . . . You look down at your feet, and you see that they are not even touching the stairs . . . You have grown so relaxed that you are now floating down . . . and down . . . relaxing deeper . . . and deeper . . . You are surprised at how free you feel . . . and you begin to understand that with relaxation comes freedom to open to wondrous things . . . 2 . . . You can see the bottom of the stairs below you now . . . You relax even more deeply as you float softly towards it . . . It is such a soothing sensation . . . to be free of the pull of gravity . . . to be free of the weight of the physical . . . You never knew you could feel so relaxed . . . 1 . . . Ever so gently your feet touch the

ground . . . You are completely relaxed and so very comfortable in each and every way . . . "
(Pause briefly here for about 15 to 30 seconds.)

"See yourself standing in a large circular room . . . As you look about you, you see that there is a large, full-length mirror in the middle of it . . . You step over to it, still thrilled at how light your steps are . . . As you stand before the mirror, you see your own reflection . . . You are amazed at how much better you look when you are relaxed . . . As you look into that mirror, the image distorts, and you see a reflection of yourself as you were five years ago . . . You remember what you were doing then . . . The image is so strong that you try to touch it, but it shifts and disappears . . ." *(Pause.)*

"Another image appears, and you see yourself 15 years ago . . . Look at the clothes . . . Remember those styles . . . Remember what you were doing then . . . *(Pause briefly.)* . . . The image shifts yet again, and you see a reflection of yourself when you were in high school . . . Notice your hair . . . Notice the clothes . . . What memories does it stir about that time in your life? . . . " *(Pause.)*

"Remembering relaxes you even more deeply . . . As you watch the images shift and change, you know that this mirror is showing you reflections of what has helped shape the you that you are now ... *(Pause.)* ... The image blurs once more and then forms a reflection of you on your first day of school ... What are you wearing? ... What are you feeling? ... How is your family acting? ... How do you feel as you step into the classroom?" *(Pause.)*

"The image shifts again, disappearing ... You breathe deeply, relaxed ... These images make you feel even more comfortable and relax you even more deeply ... The mirror fills with a myriad of swirling colors ... As they shift and dance, you feel yourself relaxing deeper ... and deeper ... feeling more comfortable ... The swirling colors shift and a vague image begins to form ... The image is distant, and you know it is not from any memory in your present life ... You watch as the image crystallizes ... You place your hand upon your cheek, unsure of what is happening ... and even though the image is vague, it mimics your movement ... And you realize this image is you, but it is a you from the past ... Slowly, softly, the image forms before you ..." *(Pause.)*

"Now I am going to ask you questions about this image, and with each question you will relax even more deeply and the image will become even more clear ... Trust your impressions ... I will pause after each question to allow your impressions to crystallize fully ... Imagine the reflection before you ... See it, feel it and know it is real . . . Is it a male or a female figure? . . . What are the clothes like? . . . Do the clothes indicate a financial or social standing? . . . What area of the world is reflected? . . . What is the primary emotion felt by the reflection? . . . Is this person happy, sad, fulfilled? . . . Do the costume and clothes reveal a particular time frame in which this life occurred? . . . What was the greatest accomplishment of that life? . . . What was the greatest failure? . . . What was not resolved and is affecting you in the present? . . .

"As you look upon this image and its background, you find you are still deeply relaxed . . . Take a few moments to study the image and discover how it is affecting you now and who else from that life is reflected within your present . . . " (Pause for three to five minutes to allow the memories to reveal themselves, and then move on to the script for the last phase.)

Part Four—Termination and Emergence
"As you look upon the images within this mirror, you realize that even further significances will reveal themselves in the days ahead . . . You find that you are still relaxed and comfortable, even with these new discoveries . . . The image blurs and you see yourself standing before your own modern-day reflection . . . You breathe deeply, relaxed and comfortable . . . Now in a few moments I am going to count from one to three so that, by the time I say num-

ber three, you will be able to open your eyes and feel wide awake . . . You will remember all that you have experienced . . . You will awaken to even further insight . . . You will feel full of pep and energy . . . You will feel invigorated and revitalized . . . You will be rejuvenated and rested . . . as though you have taken a long peaceful nap . . . You will be in complete harmony . . . You will feel fitter . . . better . . . and stronger . . . fitter . . . better . . . and stronger in every way . . . Because you have been able to relax so deeply and soundly, your mind will be sharp and alert . . . You will be able to think more clearly and creatively . . . We'll begin . . . 1 . . . You are feeling very rested now . . . Your entire body is very much at peace . . . You have been able to relax deeply and soundly and it has been this ability which has enabled you to awaken past life memories . . . In the future you will find that each session will be even more relaxing and even more rewarding . . . 2 . . . You begin to feel energy and life flowing to every part of your body now . . . The blood is beginning to circulate to your arms . . . your legs . . . your torso . . . You begin to feel strong . . . alive . . . full of energy and vigor . . . You remember all that you have experienced . . . and even more insight will reveal itself in the days ahead . . . You feel alert and awake . . . You feel perfect . . . emotionally perfect . . . physically perfect . . . mentally and spiritually perfect . . . You have

a deep feeling of well being and a tie to the past
... You feel sound ... healthier ... ready to take
on whatever may come your way ... Your eyes
feel refreshed and rested as though awakening
from a long nap ... 3 ... Your entire body, mind
and soul are refreshed ... Now open your eyes
feeling good and full of wonder and joy."

8

Dowsing Your Past Lives

The *Random House Dictionary of the English Language* defines dowsing as "searching for underground supplies of water, metal, and so on by the use of a divining rod," but this does not define the more subtle aspects of this ancient art. The art of dowsing appears originally to have had its strongest acceptance among the grass-roots people of many nations, and many today have an image of a man walking through a field with a forked stick held out in his hands. Today, though, it is enjoying a wonderful rebirth and much wider acceptance. And its image is changing.

Most states have chapters of the American Society for Dowsers. In many ways these chapters serve as a bridge between those in the psychic world and those within the scientific community. In more recent times dowsing has moved beyond merely searching for water sources. Dowsing has been taught to power company employees to assist them in digging up appropriate power lines. It was also taught as a method of mine detection to groups involved in the Vietnam conflict.

Dowsing has been called by many names—water witching, water divining and so on. It has been in evidence throughout recorded history. Some dowsers suggest that Moses's staff with which he struck a rock and caused water to come forth (Exodus 17) was simply an example of dowsing.

"The earliest existing illustration of dowsing after the invention of printing (circa 1454) is dated 1550 and portrays seven workmen mining, breaking up, and hauling away ore while a dowser with a forked stick prospects the ground above for fresh deposits . . . and *De Re Metallica* (1556) by G. Agricola also depicts mining, showing in one sketch no fewer than five dowsers at work."*

Although there had always been a veil of secrecy and mystery around dowsing and the use of divining rods, this veil disintegrated in modern times. People from all walks of life are beginning to work with dowsing for everything from locating water to finding missing people to discovering power points upon the planet to healing and even discovering past lives.

---

*Howell, Harvey. *Dowsing for Everyone*. Vermont: The Stephen Green Press, 1979, p. 12.

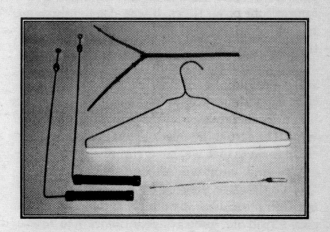

COMMON DOWSING INSTRUMENTS

There is still a great deal of mystery about how dowsing works. Some believe it is simply an involuntary muscle reaction to an outside impulse, springing from the earth or some other source. Others hold the view that it is entirely psychic in its nature. In this case, the divining rod simply helps you to attune to your own extrasensory perception.

Most of the early rods were wood. The most commonly used kind of wood was hazel. For this reason the divining rod was often called the "witch hazel." In truth the wooden rods can be taken from any tree as long as they are in a "Y" shape and about two feet long. Today dowsing instruments vary in shape and the material of which they are constructed. They can be wood, plastic or metal. There are L-rods and a variety of pendulums, and even simple coat hangers can be used as effective dowsing instruments.

Dowsing rods provide a link to our intuitive side. They are an extension of our eyes, providing visual clues that we can more easily recognize than pure intuition. Although some dowsers would disagree, the rods have no special quality of their own. They are simply tools to heighten our sensitivity. Almost anyone can learn to dowse as long as we approach it with an open mind.

Radiesthesia is the more scientific name for dowsing. In our technological society, there is a tendency to accept things as more legitimate if they are given a scientific label. All radiesthesia is, though, is divining or dowsing an energy radiation. It involves using an instrument to locate or determine the strength of a particular radiation.

Dowsing rods assist us to communicate with levels of our mind that have the capability to recognize the subtle energy fields we encounter or cross within our lives. We are constantly interacting with outside energies, be they the energies of others or the various energies that comprise the earth and the sky. Most of the time we are not conscious of this interaction and so we do not acknowledge it.

The subconscious mind does register these interactions, no matter how subtle they are. The dowsing tools simply help us to communicate with our subconscious more effectively. Through them we awaken our greater powers of perception. The dowsing tools become an extension of our subconscious. They are a link between the nervous system (and the subconscious mind working through it) and the energy fields we interact with. The nervous system sends electrical signals and impulses that cause the dowsing instrument to move.

This is especially noticeable in the case of the pendulum. The swinging of the pendulum is an ideomotor response. It is caused by involuntary muscle action stimulated by the subconscious mind through the sympathetic nervous system.

The nervous system is our internal communication network. It sends us signals and messages from the various levels of our mind. Radiesthesia devices (dowsing instruments) amplify those signals, enabling us to detect them more easily and translate them.

To apply dowsing to past life discovery, we must understand some simple aspects of human energy. You are an energy system. You give off and are comprised of a wide variety of energy emanations and fields. These include, but are not limited to, light, sound, electricity, magnetism, heat and so on. You leave traces of your energy wherever you go. The more sustained your contact with a particular area, the stronger your energy affects it.

An easy example to help you understand this effect is to think back on your childhood. Do you remember how your parents' room felt? Do you remember how it had a different feel about it than your room or your brother's or sister's room? We each have our own unique energy, and our energy affects the areas in which we live and the people within our lives in very subtle but real ways.

The theory in past life discovery is that we have left strong energy traces at points in time and space where we have had other lives. When we dowse for those past lives, we are using our tools to attune to those distant traces. Just as migrating birds make and follow a particular path that they can recognize, our lives have also followed a track. And there are markers that we can use to trace the course of our own journey. Those markers are our past lives.

This idea of paths or traces is similar to the concept of ley lines that has gained so much attention in recent times. A ley line is "an invisible source of energy that comes from on high, makes a 90 degree turn when it touches the ground and then proceeds along the surface for a distance before entering the earth."* The point

---

*Howell, Harvey. *Dowsing for Everyone*. Vermont: The Stephen Green Press, 1979, p. 74.

where it touches the earth is a power center. "Early Pagans in what is now Britain established their cells on power centers located by some strange divination. Then Druids took over, adopting the same sites . . . Eventually Christianity arrived and the altar was replaced by the baptismal font, the water in which was rendered holy by the divine power of the ley line descending on it."**

Our times on the physical plane can be likened to the flow of these ley lines and their corresponding power centers. Each of our lives creates a power point upon the earth in the area where we lived. Through dowsing, we can attune to those points.

Sample Time Line

In the sample time line below, an asterisk [*] indicates a point in time where you may have left a trace of your energy. Like a ley line, we enter into the physical and follow a course of life. That point at which we connect back into earth life is a power point. It reflects a past life, and such points can be dowsed.

```
_____ * * _____ * _____ * _____ * _
3000 B.C.        1000 B.C.   B.C. A.D.  1000 A.D.
```

THE BRONZE AGE   ANCIENT EMPIRES   THE DARK AGES

**Ibid., pp. 74-75.

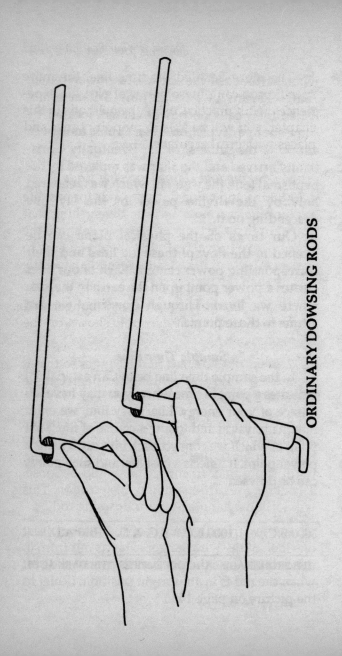

ORDINARY DOWSING RODS

The more detailed the time line, the more specific you can dowse points of past life experiences. With practice, using the methods in this chapter, you will be able to pinpoint times and places with great accuracy.

Making and Using Dowsing Rods

Making and using dowsing rods for past life exploration is simple and fun. Everything that you need to make them can be found around the home. These instructions will show you how to make two sets of L-Rods, the second just a little fancier than the first.

1. Take an ordinary wire coat hanger and make two cuts in it at the spots shown on the followingpage.

2. Bend the side part of the hanger so that it is completely vertical, forming a 90 degree angle with the bottom.

3. Cut a piece of cardboard the size of the small side of the L-shaped hanger. Roll it up tight enough so that it will fit over the hanger, but it should *not* fit snugly. It should be loose. Then tape the cardboard into this position. This will form the handle for your dowsing rod.

4. Now trim the cardboard so that at least one inch of the wire hanger extends out from it. Bend this over so that the handle cannot slide off when the rod is in an upright position. (Refer to the picture on page 145.)

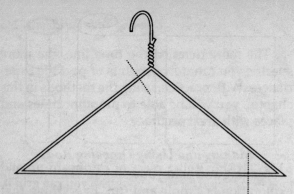

STEP ONE: Using an ordinary coat hanger, make two cuts in it as indicated in the above picture.

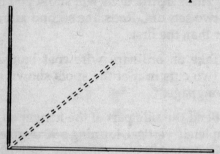

STEP TWO: Bend the side portion of the hanger upright. It stands vertically at a 90-degree angle.

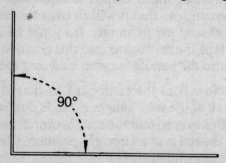

MAKING ORDINARY DOWSING RODS

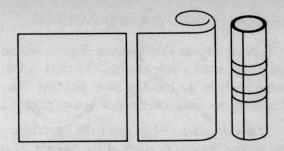

STEP THREE: Roll a piece of cardboard up and tape it. It should be stiff enough so you can grip it, and it should loosely fit over the vertical bar of the hanger.

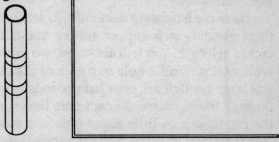

STEPS FOUR AND FIVE: Slide the cardboard handle over the vertical bar, so that at least one inch sticks out. Bend this over to keep the cardboard on. Turn the rod upright.

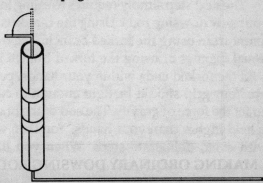

5. Now repeat this process with a second hanger to create a pair of rods. The rods should swing freely in the handles when finished. They should appear similar to those shown on page 142.

Many dry-cleaner hangers have a cardboard roll on the bottom portion of the hanger. This can be removed, cut and used as an effective grip. A more intricate version can also be constructed with inexpensive materials from any hardware store:

Have the hardware store cut two sections of three-quarter–inch copper tubing about five inches in length. You will also need two caps for each section. Drill a hole into each of the caps, just large enough for your hanger rods to pass through freely. Fasten the caps onto the ends of the cut tubing. A little super glue will insure that they stay in place. Slide the rods through the handles so that about an inch extends out the bottom. Bend this slightly, and you have a stronger, more durable L-rod.

The next step simply requires learning to use your new dowsing rods. Using the L-rods is different from using the forked branch. The traditional manner of using the forked branch is to hold the forked ends within your hands, palms up. Your grip should be tight enough to counteract the force of gravity. The end of the branch is held higher than your hands. You then walk with even, deliberate steps. When you draw close to what you are searching for, the point should bow down.

In a traditional search, the L-rods could be used in the same manner. They would be held at waist level, elbows at the side. The points should be held slightly down, providing gravitational resistance to lateral movement. When the energy source is found, the ends of the L-rods will either swing open, or they will cross. It will vary from individual to individual.

The first thing to do is to become comfortable with the feel of your rods and how they work. Develop a mindset as to how you expect the rods to respond. What do you want an outward swinging motion to indicate? What do you want a crossing of the rods to indicate? Determine this ahead of time and hold to this every time you use them. For some people, the swinging open of the rods can indicate an affirmative or "yes" response, and a crossing can indicate a negative or "no" response.

Program the rods to work for you. Hold them in front of you and think to yourself the word "YES." Focus on this until the rods swing in the manner you have decided for "yes." Then do the same for "NO." Ask a series of simple yes-and-no questions.

With much of the dowsing work, you must learn to ask yourself yes and no questions. The more specific, the better. For example, you may ask the rods or pendulum if a certain food is

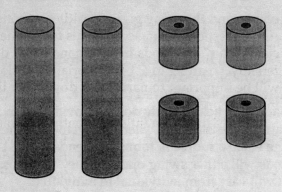

Begin with small sections of copper tubing and copper caps to fit over the ends. Drill holes in the caps so the rods will fit through.

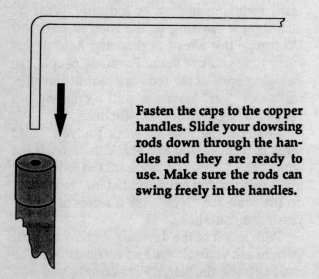

Fasten the caps to the copper handles. Slide your dowsing rods down through the handles and they are ready to use. Make sure the rods can swing freely in the handles.

MAKING DURABLE DOWSING RODS

edible, and they may give a positive response. If the question is phrased, "Is this food beneficial for me," your rods may respond much differently. Learning to ask appropriate questions will be important to narrowing down past life information.

L-rods are used a little differently from their traditional manner when dowsing for past lives. One L-rod can be used as a directional finder. You will also need some maps. One of the simplest ways of dowsing past lives is to hold the end of the L-rod over a map and allow it to point out the general area of a past life now affecting you. Also, by slowly moving the L-rod across the face of the map, the end will stabilize and move to those points associated with your question: "Where did I have a past life that is currently affecting me?"

Make sure you use an appropriate question. Such questions as "Where did I have a past life that is currently affecting me?" or "Where should I start my past life exploration" or "Point out the area of an important past life" are effective.

You can also construct your own dowsing charts for this, such as those on the following two pages. Begin by determining the continent by using either the full map or the sample diagram on page 150. Then narrow down the country by getting a more specific map or by constructing a chart that has the countries listed for each continent. If you wish to pursue this

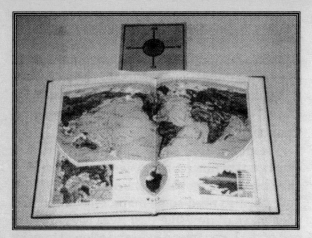

Using maps and charts, you can ask the L-rod to point in the direction of a past life that is currently affecting you. You can construct your maps and charts with varying degrees of intricacy to narrow down the location. With practice, you will be able to recognize the subtle play of past lives through your dowsing instrument.

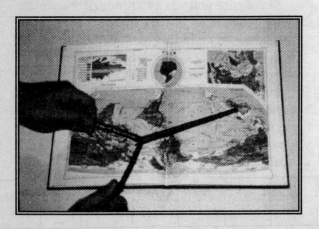

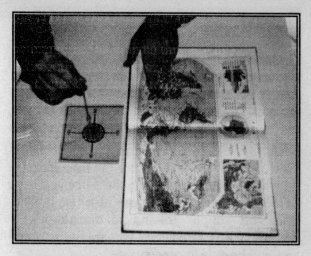

ANY DOWSING INSTRUMENT, EVEN A PENDULUM, CAN HELP US LOCATE TIMES AND PLACES OF PAST LIVES THAT ARE CURRENTLY AFFECTING US

600 A.D.	700 A.D.	800 A.D.	900 A.D.	1000 A.D.	1100 A.D.	1200 A.D.

seriously, you could begin a file of maps and charts that can be used for past life exploration through dowsing.

Once you have narrowed down the place, begin to work on the period of time. Construct a time chart, as simple or as intricate as you find desirable. (See the sample on page 141.) Hold your L-rod over it and ask for the time frame in which you had a past life in the place you have already determined. You can also use both L-rods and simple yes-and-no questioning to determine this. Make sure you are undisturbed and will be able to concentrate.

1. Begin by asking the L-rod to point in the direction of a past life now affecting you. Then narrow it down using more specific maps.

2. Next determine the time frame of the life you spent in the area dowsed. You can use a specific chart or simply ask specific questions, once the century is determined. For example, if you dowsed a past life in France in the 14th century, hold both L-rods and ask questions such as, "Was I born in 1310?" "1320?" and so on. Remember that dowsing instruments respond to yes and no questions.

3. Next, through the questioning procedure, explore the details of that life:

— Was I male or female?
— Was I rich?

— Was I married?
— Did I have a family?
— Did I have one child? two? three?
— Did I make my living in a trade?
— Are any members of that family part of my present life?
— Are they part of my present family?

Ask as many questions and get as specific as you can. Write down the answers in your Past Life Journal. With practice you will be able to identify places, periods and people from your past within your present. You will be able to identify lessons, if any, that may be associated with them.

4. The dowsing will not provide all of the answers, but it will provide enough so that you can, through meditation and reflection, put many aspects of your present life into a new perspective.

Dowsing Past Lives with Pendulums

The pendulum was born from the dowsing tradition. A pendulum will work along the same lines and principles as any other dowsing instrument. The swinging of the pendulum provides clues that can be used to draw answers from the subconscious mind.

Pendulums can be made from simple objects around the home. Buttons, rings and crystals are commonly used. The best pendulums, though,

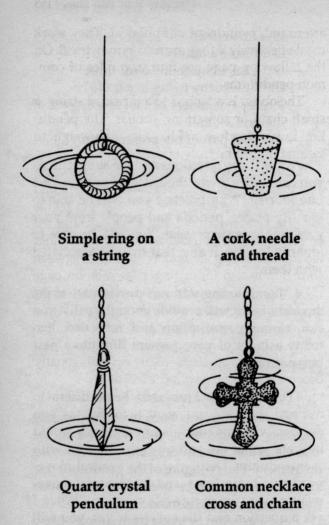

**Simple ring on
a string**

**A cork, needle
and thread**

**Quartz crystal
pendulum**

**Common necklace
cross and chain**

COMMON TYPES OF PENDULUMS

are round, cylindrical or spherical. They work most effectively if they are also symmetrical. On the following page are four examples of common pendulums.

The object is attached to a thread, a string, a small chain or something similar. The pendulum must hang free and have enough weight to swing if it is to be truly effective.

Learning to use a pendulum or any dowsing instrument is easy. It requires only a little time and practice in a quiet place. The first step is to get the feel of it. Sit at a desk or table. Place your feet flat on the floor. Rest your elbow on the desk. Hold the pendulum by the end of its chain between your thumb and index finger (as seen on page 151). Allow it to hang for a moment or two to get the feel of its weight. Now circle it gently in a clockwise direction. Allow it to stop and then rotate it in a counterclockwise direction. Next move it vertically, horizontally and diagonally. Become comfortable with the feel of it.

The next step is to program the pendulum to respond the way you want it to. Just as you decided what movements of the L-rods would indicate yes or no, you must do likewise with the pendulum. Decide whether vertical movement is to indicate yes and a horizontal movement no, or vice versa. Tell yourself, "When I ask a question and the answer is yes, you will make the pendulum move [direction]." Do the same for the no response.

Take a few minutes a day to work and experiment with your pendulum. Remember you are programming your subconscious to provide tangible input through the movement of the pendulum. The direction of the movement, as well as its intensity and speed, will all have meaning.

For past life exploration, use the pendulum with the maps and charts just as you did with the L-rod. In the example at the top of page 154, direct the pendulum to point out a continent upon which you lived in the past in a life that is currently affecting you. Focus. Concentrate upon the question. Repeat it over and over in your mind. The direction of the pendulum's swing will provide the answer. If the swing is not strong or clear, simply hold the pendulum over each continent in turn and ask the question: "Did I have a past life here that is currently affecting me?" Then narrow it down further from the continent to the country and so on.

Dates can be determined the same way. Once the place and time is determined, begin the more in-depth questioning, just as you learned to do with the L-rods. Focus and try to define specific problem patterns, sources and possible solutions. Refer to #3 on pages 152-153. With practice you will be able to locate and define past life connections and their relationships to present life circumstances. Record your results in your Past Life Journal.

9

Rites of Passage

Any discussion of past lives would be incomplete without some reflection upon the two greatest mysteries of life—birth and death. Birth and death are the greatest changes we encounter, but they are not the only ones. Change occurs on many levels and at many different times in our lives. Changes are blessings. They are signal flares of new growth, but we must take responsibility for our individual lives and their circumstances upon all levels in order to appreciate the blessing of a change.

Part of the initiatory process in many of the ancient traditions involved symbolic births and deaths—*rites of passage*. The student of the mysteries would symbolically die to one stage of his or her life to be reborn into yet a new one. This was a rite of passage. Rebirth could not occur without death.

A rite of passage is often a celebration of a transition in one's life, and variations of some ancient ones are still practiced today. The Jewish Bar Mitzvah is an example of the rite of passage of a boy into manhood. Baptisms and dedications at birth are rites of passage; they honor and acknowledge the transition from the spiritual to the physical. Funerals are also rites of passage in that they assist the soul in making the transition from the physical to the spiritual once again. Our entire time within the physical plane can be seen as an extended rite of passage.

We are all being challenged to let go of the old and create the new. Each of us in our own way is challenged by our life circumstances to learn new aspects of the universal lesson of life and death. We are each learning to give up the old and initiate the new, so each physical life can be seen as a rite of passage to new heights.

If we are to take advantage of the opportunities that such an experience in the physical can create, we must expand our awareness of life and its processes. We must begin to look at the world as energy in various forms. We must learn how energy operates within our lives. We must recognize that we are spirit in our truest essence. And if we can do something as magnificent as take upon ourselves a physical body, then certainly we can learn to manifest greater love, prosperity, fulfillment and abundance within our short times upon the earth.

The body is not the whole person. It is a vehicle, and yet it is essential, for it will be the focus and beneficiary of our thoughts, deeds, actions and emotions. Its health and abilities will depend upon its right use and care, life after life. We use the physical body to assist us in evolving.

The foundations of our physical, emotional, mental and spiritual health are laid before birth— even before conception. The child is born into a home according to parental perceptions, heredity and environment, past life and karmic ties and the strength of prayer, attitude and meditation.

The processes of being born and dying are complex. We need to encounter a number of experiences before we can attain to our highest potential. We choose an environment for birth that will challenge and teach us how to create within the world in the manner of the divine that lives within us. Then we move on to prepare for the next opportunity.

Our development and growth follow two strands after the moment of conception. We begin to develop from the body up and from the spirit down. (Refer to the diagram on page 6.) We are all dual, an immortal spirit in a mortal body.

Although we come into this world as a child, the true self is wise and developed. This spiritual aspect is the result of vast experience, much of which has been gained through successive births in other physical bodies. The fruits of those previous lives become the eternal possession of the soul. With each new incarnation, we bring the seeds of those faculties with us. Those faculties, though, must be re-awakened, redeveloped and further expanded upon, while we also work to attain new capacities.

Remember that, even if you developed an ability or faculty in the past, it does not mean that it will be easily and immediately awakened in the present. It is a seed that you bring with you into each incarnation to nurture into new growth. We have, of course, free will, so whether or not we use those seeds is entirely up to us.

This is comparable to an individual who learned to do a gymnastic back flip as a child. Once it was learned, the person stopped, never again exercising, stretching or practicing that move. Then 30 years later this individual attempts to do that same back flip, assuming it will be easy because he or she did it as a child. The potential for injury is tremendous. Any faculty developed in the past must be redeveloped, restrengthened and expressed appropriately within the conditions of the present.

Yes, there are exceptions. We often see this in child prodigies. But even in these cases, there must still be development, discipline, nurturing and proper expression. If we place a child in the center of a room and yell at it and tell it that it is ugly and stupid and clumsy, it will respond in one of two ways. It will either withdraw into itself and never realize its full potential or it will become a holy terror. If we take that same child and place it in the middle of the room and tell it that we love it, that it is beautiful, that it is okay to make mistakes when we're growing and learning, the potential that could unfold—the fruits of the past that could manifest—would be staggering.

Our pasts cannot be changed, but the future is being shaped by our current rite of passage. Birth and death are the rituals that begin and end our passage in our physical existence. If we can change our perspectives on birth and death, a new reverence for ourselves, our world and our inherent, infinite potential arises. When we change our imaginings, we change our world!

The Mysteries of Birth*

"And a woman who held a babe against her bosom said, Speak to us of children.

"And he said:

"Your children are not your children.

"They are the sons and daughters of Life's longing for itself.

"They come through you but not from you,

"And they are with you yet they belong not to you.

---

*Many esoteric groups, clairvoyants and seers have described the hidden and subtle aspects of birth and death. Although not truly verified, they explain much of what has often been unexplainable. These spiritual aspects provide a different perspective into the magnificent wonders of these mysteries, and they assist us in understanding the dynamic processes involved in the reincarnation process. These descriptions are a synthesis of various teachings on the subjects. For more specific information, consult the sources listed in the bibliography.

"You may give them your love but not your thoughts,

"For they have their own thoughts.

"You may house their bodies but not their souls,

"For their souls dwell in the house of tomorrow which you cannot visit, not even in your dreams.

"You may strive to be like them, but seek not to make them like you.

"For life goes not backward nor tarries with yesterday."*

At the moment of conception, the spiritual essence begins to work toward attuning itself to what will eventually become the physical body. Our spiritual essence has too intense an energy for it to instantly link with anything physical; thus it is done in stages throughout the nine-month pregnancy. Subtle bands of energy are built around the soul essence to soften and filter its influence upon the physical vehicle so that it can more easily align and integrate fully with the it at or around the time of birth.

This is accomplished with the assistance of those beings often described as the angelic hierarchy. This group includes, but is not limited to, the archangels, angels, devas, nature spirits and

*From *The Prophet* by Kahlil Gibran, copyright 1923 by Kahlil Gibran and renewed 1951 by Administrators C.T.A. of Kahlil Gibran estate and Mary G. Gibran. Reprinted by permission of Alfred A. Knopf, Inc., 1951.

elementals. Most humans still relegate these beings to the realm of fiction and fairy tale, especially in this age of intellectual and scientific focus.

The angelic hierarchy is just as real as we are, only without physical bodies. They have bodies of lighter substance that are mostly invisible to our self-limiting perceptions. We exist in a living universe, and most of the good we know—be it the beauty of nature, the gift of birth or the wonders and blessings of life—we owe to these beings.

Humanity is smug. We like to believe that we are the highest form of life. We do have a divine spark, but so do countless other life forms. And there are many more that express that divine spark much more radiantly and consistently than we do. Our consciousness is broadened by considering the existence of beings unlike us in physical appearance but one with us in service to the divine forces of the universe. The wonders and miracles of life—physical and spiritual—open to us when we learn to recognize, reverence and love both the visible and invisible realms of life.

In birth these beings help construct our new bodies, subtle and physical, and they help the ego of our soul to integrate with that new body. In death they assist in the withdrawal from the physical vehicle and the disintegration of its form and energy.

Their first tasks begin at conception. A sphere of influence to help insulate the developing fetus is established. The womb of the mother is magnetized and attuned. The energy system of the mother, especially in the womb area, must be brought into vibrational harmony with the energy of the soul about to incarnate. Until this harmony is established, the mother experiences "morning sickness."

To a great degree the amount of harmony that can be established within the sphere of the mother and child helps to determine the quality of the physical form. This is also influenced by karmic law and genetics. Thus, if there is something that the soul has chosen to encounter physically during the upcoming incarnation, a predisposition to a weakness in that area may result. It doesn't mean that it will manifest, but it may simply be a predisposition, a physical reminder to the soul that something is out of balance.

The chakra system is adjusted and attuned to the physical glands and nervous system, as well as to levels of consciousness. The chakras mediate all energy coming into and going out of the body. They tie the subtle bodies to the physical so that integration of the true spiritual essence can occur.

Each chakra is attuned to specific functions and seed capabilities, according to the karma of the individual. Again—depending upon what has been accomplished in the past, what lessons

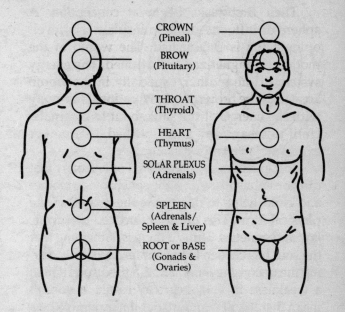

CROWN
(Pineal)

BROW
(Pituitary)

THROAT
(Thyroid)

HEART
(Thymus)

SOLAR PLEXUS
(Adrenals)

SPLEEN
(Adrenals/
Spleen & Liver)

ROOT or BASE
(Gonads &
Ovaries)

THE CHAKRA SYSTEM

The chakras mediate all energy within, coming into and going out of the body. They help distribute energy for our physical, emotional, mental and spiritual functions.

The chakras are attuned to a particular seed level of function, according to the past karma of the individual. The task of the individual is to reawaken and expand upon that level.

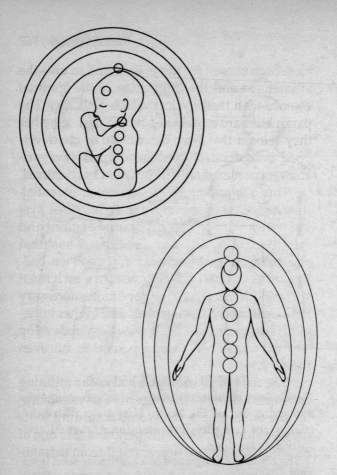

Depending upon genetics, karma and what we have chosen to take upon ourselves in this incarnation, the chakras
and our subtle bodies develop and align with the physical in varying degrees of harmony. This alignment reflects
the physical, emotional, mental and spiritual weaknesses,
abilities, and potentials we must learn to work with. As we
grow and develop, we can activate and align our energies
more fully, allowing the seeds of birth to flower.

have been chosen for the present and so on—the attunement and the integration of the spiritual essence with the physical vehicle will vary. The parameters are established by the past. Whether they remain that way, deteriorate or are developed and extended will depend upon other variables encountered once incarnation has occurred.

This alignment is the inherent potential. Remember, though, that we come into the physical to test our abilities to remain balanced and creative under all circumstances. Thus that alignment is easily altered for good or bad. Regardless of past development, we each must still win for ourselves the conditions necessary for heightened consciousness and higher initiation. This means we must reawaken, redevelop and express those energy potentials on even higher levels.

The first three months involve the attuning and constructing of the pattern of physical form for the fetus within the womb according to its own unique purpose. This period is also one of creating some insulation about it from extraneous energies.

While this is occurring on the physical level, the spiritual essence (with the assistance of the angelic hierarchy) is building the subtle bodies that will filter its intense vibration and facilitate its ultimate union with the physical vehicle. From the moment of conception, a link between our spiritual essence and our developing physical vehicle is formed. This link increases over the nine-month pregnancy.

During the first four months, a number of the angelic hierarchy work to protect the mother from adverse circumstances. Since the embryo shares in the energy of the mother, this is even more important. Nature spirits work to assist in vitalizing the embryo. This is often when the first kicks begin to be felt. Members of the angelic hierarchy draw closer and more protective around the mother. This accounts for that special "glow."

From the fifth through the eighth month, a more direct alignment of the spiritual essence with the fetus occurs. This is a time during which communication with the fetus by the mother and the father should increase, because it will be more receptive. By the eighth month, a good measure of consciousness has aligned with the physical body. This increases daily from this time on.

In the case of a premature birth, the development and alignment occurs outside of the mother's body. The angelic hierarchy and the nature spirits strive to complete their alignment outside the protective environment of the womb. Their numbers increase, as do their efforts. To many, this accounts for the often "fairy-like" appearance of premature babies.

Just prior to birth, the angels and nature spirits withdraw. Their efforts now are focused on stabilizing the subtle bodies through the pain of birth. The complete union of the spiritual essence and the new physical body can occur at any time after conception, but most frequently it occurs around the actual time of birth. Once that first breath is taken and the body is separated from the mother, then it becomes a distinct entity and begins its own unique work.

Throughout the pregnancy the soul hovers about the mother and the developing body while those of the angelic kingdom work to manifest a new opportunity for incarnation. The more we heed this, the more awareness will grow of the soul that is incarnating. Mother and father both should pay close attention to dreams throughout the pregnancy, as they often reveal much about the incarnating soul. They also often reveal past life information and connections to this soul.

There should be prayer, meditation and conversation with the incarnating soul throughout the pregnancy. Send welcoming thoughts and love to it. Include the angels and nature spirits assisting in the process, whether you are consciously aware of their presence or not. Adapt the previous past life meditations to discovering your relationship with this new child. Simply look into the picture and allow the image of the new child to reveal itself behind your own image. Visualize the image of the past becoming one of the present in which you lovingly embrace this child. This will aid in understanding the nature of the incoming child and your past life connections to it. It will keep alive the beauty, wonder and divinity of creation.

The Mystery of Death

Death is the unfathomable mystery, the shadowy figure wearing a cowled robe. Many myths show death as the grim reaper or the fearful coachman. Death has come in many guises and yet, when understood, holds the key to immortality.

Humanity has always regarded death with great awe and fear. All of the ancient civilizations had ritualized procedures and concepts concerning this process. Many of the ancient religions utilized specific procedures to assist the individual in finding the way through the veils surrounding death. The Egyptians and Tibetans often buried their dead with manuals so that the soul could find its way through the underworld.

There has always been a fear of death. It is an unknown, and it separates us from those we love. People fear death because it may cut short careers, ambitions and desires. People fear death because of religious reasons as well: being plunged into a Purgatory for purification or into an eternal Hell does little to ease this primal fear.

Through the study of reincarnation, we come to realize that the physical body is just a temporary housing for our true self. Death is not the dying of the self or the cessation of our spirit. Death is a separation of the higher and lower principles within us. It is the shedding of the physical so that we can assimilate our learnings and prepare for even greater lessons.

Death serves many functions. It provides a release from the burdens of the flesh. It provides a release from suffering. It provides opportunities to learn for those who are left behind. It provides opportunities to transition to yet higher states of consciousness.

There are two kinds of death, natural and unnatural. A natural death is a gradual unloosening of the energy fabric of the soul from the physical. A natural death occurs when the karma of the incarnation has been accomplished. It is always peaceful.

The second kind of passing is the unnatural. This is death involving disease, illness, pathology, accident, suicide and so on. It can be peaceful or unpeaceful. Dying from most disease is not a natural death, although there can be exceptions. Illness and disease often reflect an imbalance or disharmony within some aspect of life's processes.

We can all learn to pass out of physical life in full consciousness. It is often said that the adept dies as he or she has lived—serenely. Although some may think it morbid, this awareness begins with simple meditation upon death. Studying the withdrawal process and visualizing the shedding of your physical and subtle bodies is a great help. Take time to image the life you will lead after this one. Take time periodically to review your life in reverse. Start with where you are now and look back over the events to the time of birth. Visualize and imagine yourself meeting and communicating with loved ones who have passed on before you. See it as a transition and not as an end.

As the time of the death transition draws near, the soul begins preparations for its withdrawal. The cessation of physical life triggers the reverse of what occurred in the manifestation after conception. The consciousness withdraws from the physical into the subtle bodies and each in turn is disentangled and disintegrated.

How long this takes will vary from individual to individual. The first step is disentangling from the physical plane and adjusting to the etheric level. This usually only takes a short time. Anyone who has ever attended a funeral that was preceded by a viewing will have recognized a noticeable difference in the appearance of the body even in a short 24 hour period. As the subtle life force is disentangled and withdrawn to the etheric level, the physical vehicle will reflect the effects.

Although the soul cannot take possession of the physical body again, it is familiar with that body. Often, while in the etheric band of energy, the soul will stay close to the physical body.

Sometimes it does this to provide comfort to those left behind. Sometimes it just does not realize that it is no longer part of physical life. In the latter case, frantic efforts may be made to restore touch with the physical. This is where we get our "ghosts in the graveyard" or appearances in old "haunts" of their physical life.

No soul passes unaided. If it is a peaceful passing, relatives and loved ones who have already passed on will usually gather to assist.

Those who die without the natural opportunity to prepare, such as in the case of war or accident, may reincarnate for just a brief time to make a more natural transition. I have heard some espouse the theory that this explains the infant death syndrome.

Others who pass unexpectedly—through accident or even suicide—have assistance. A group of the angelic hierarchy sometimes called the Watchers, the Angels of the Night or by some other name work to insure that no soul transits without assistance. These beings are considered the most loving of all the angelic beings, for those who do pass suddenly or by suicide need a special love and nurturing to face what has occurred.

Most of our funeral customs have an esoteric aspect that is linked to the concept of life after death. As mentioned, after the cessation of physical life, the soul remains close to the physical body to untangle all threads. The soul is now cut off from the prana or life force that it would normally draw from the sun through the physical body. Thus it draws energy from other sources. This is why candles are lit and flowers are placed about. They provide enough subtle energy vibrations for the disentangling to be completed. They also prevent energy from being zapped and drawn from the living.

Many people avoid funerals because of the strange feelings associated with them. Most of the time the feelings do not originate with us. Usually they come from one of three sources. First, as the soul withdraws from the physical, so does the archangel which watches over that soul. This creates a definite feeling of emptiness.

Also, the elemental kingdoms are activated. Their energy is very strong and often quite tangible. They are always present and active when organic matter needs to be animated or disintegrated. People at funerals often feel their presence, not knowing what it is.

The third source for many strange feelings at funerals is the presence of those who have already passed. Friends, relatives and loved ones no longer in the physical will gather to assist the newly deceased soul and to help provide comfort to those still in the physical.

Although black is often considered the color of death, it is very insulating. It protects and prevents oversensitivity to these subtle energy plays that manifest at funerals.

As the soul withdraws from the physical, it begins the process of evaluation and assimilation of its life experiences. It begins to make preparations to return once more for yet further lessons. It grows in its awareness that we are never separate from those we love. We begin to learn that those who have touched us, have helped create us and are forever a part of us. We learn to embrace life with joy and approach death with wonder.

"When I die
I'm sure I will have a big funeral . . .
Curiosity seekers . . .
coming to see if I am really dead . . .
Or just trying to make TROUBLE . . . "*

*Evans, Mari E. "The Rebel," *Our Own Thing*. Englewood Cliffs, NJ: Prentice Hall, 1973, p. 156.

EXERCISE:
ATTUNING TO THE INCOMING CHILD

The time of pregnancy is an excellent time to attune to the incoming soul. You can discover many past life connections, along with qualities and characteristics of the child. Begin by paying attention to your dreams during this time. Often recurring emotions in the dreams can reflect the emotional connection between you and the child.

At the moment of conception, the link with the mother and the father begins. Your perceptions of this linking process may be faint and indistinct at first, but they will become more precise throughout the pregnancy. It is an excellent time to develop the faculties for spiritual perception. The following exercise will assist in this.

1. Make sure you will be undisturbed. Dim the lights and close your eyes. Rose fragrance is very beneficial for this exercise. Perform a progressive relaxation and some rhythmic breathing.

2. This exercise can be performed by one or both parents. If performed together, the mother should sit on the floor with her hands resting upon her womb. The father should sit behind and directly up against the mother. His arms should reach around and either rest upon hers or upon the womb also.

3. As you relax, see a soft light beginning to shine from your heart center. If performing this

meditation with the other parent, see the two shining together, growing stronger, uniting, entwining. From this light a soft cloud emanates before you and begins to take on a beautiful, brilliant and golden-white form. See this as your spiritual essence.

4. As you sit in this position, you observe this form raising its eyes to the distant heavens as if looking for something particular. Then you notice. It is faint at first, but then a white light gently becomes distinct in the heavens above. See it is as soft and almost beaming and twinkling down upon you.

5. From that light a soft cloud begins to descend. Visualize it. Imagine it. See how perfect and beautiful it is as it descends. It is like a small bubble of crystalline energy. Let it descend at its own speed. Don't try to force it toward you faster.

6. It hovers before your own spiritual essence. There is a brief sharing of light as in greeting, and then it moves beside your spiritual essence as if to observe you. It hovers, pulsating soft, beautiful energy. And you know that this is the spiritual essence of the soul you will give birth to.

7. Observe it. Notice the colors. Notice what feelings arise in you as you observe it. Mentally ask questions of this soul that has come to greet you:

— What physical environment will it most need to grow?
— What emotions does it stir in you?
— What sort of people will it need to be around?
— What is its purpose?
— What has it come to learn from you and to teach you?
— How can you best help it?
— Are there colors that would be beneficial for it?
— What name would be most suitable to assist it in its purpose? (Don't try to force answers. As the pregnancy continues, so will the clarity and quantity of answers.)

8. Then send feelings of love and welcome to this spiritual essence. As you do so, it floats back toward your spiritual essence. The forms and lights of both merge, uniting with an intensity of light and a shower of rainbow colors. You can almost hear the heavens singing a song of joy at the creative union. The two pulsate, sharing their energies and their essences, and they become one form.

9. This one form, shining with greater brilliance, turns to you and gently merges back within your physical body. A shiver of joy runs through you, filling you with joy and wonder. The light in your heart shines even more brightly! And then you feel it. A soft gentle pulse is felt

within your body. You are not sure if you imagined it or not, but then your hands upon the womb feel it again. And your heart leaps!

10. Breathe deeply, welcoming and rejoicing in this wonderful opportunity. Then very slowly allow your awareness to return to normal.

10

Proving Your Past Lives

It is important in past life exploration to avoid self-deception. This is best done by increasing your level of awareness and by being harshly honest. Most of the lives we remember that are affecting us now will not be famous lives. They probably will not be glamorous, exciting or dramatic. Our greatest growth comes from those lives in which we were learning to meet our daily trials and obligations.

Do not glamorize your past lives. Realize that almost all of us have had lives of great abilities, fulfillment and abundance on all levels. Most of us have also had the opposite sort of lives as well. Each life brings with it its own unique but no less important lessons.

Do not become too preoccupied with past lives. Your focus should always be in the present. If you find yourself constantly talking and describing your past lives to others or if you find yourself rushing home from work every night to do another exploration, you are losing your objectivity and you should back away from it. You may be using past life exploration as an escape from the present.

It also can be very easy to misinterpret past lives and their influences and correlations to our present life. This is one of the reasons I recommend keeping a past life journal. The act of recording forces the conscious mind to analyze and examine things a little more closely. We can also then go back periodically and review how accurate our interpretations are.

If you used the information from a past life to identify and change a pattern in your present and it did not work, you may need to rethink its true connection to the present. Is it just some subconscious fancy that emerged, some form of wishful thinking, or did you just not apply the information appropriately? Discrimination is the key. Test all things. Many times, the application of past life information to present circumstances is a trial and error process.

How do we assess the validity of the information? Even if we prove that a person with such a name lived at the time and place discovered, it does not necessarily prove you were that person. More important than proving the historic aspect of the past life discovery is to find a beneficial use for it. Does the information explain a present life situation and decrease your anxiety about it? Does the awareness help you to resolve an old problem or break a negative pattern? Does it make you feel better about yourself or someone else?

Only you can determine the validity of the information. Take no one else's word for it. Always look for an application. Part of the process of evolving means taking a more active responsibility in your life for what you allow within it. Test all things.

It is also easy to confuse bad judgment with bad karma. Trivial affairs are often excused in the name of some past life involvement. There are those who use karma to excuse or alibi every quirk or folly in the present life. Remember that we entered into a physical form to learn new things as well as to correct the old.

Remember that you do not have to be aware of the laws of evolution, reincarnation and karma to fulfill yourself and grow. Simply living a positive and creative life in the present will resolve the past and set positive patterns for the future. Living by the profound rule of "doing unto others . . .," seeking to fulfill your life's duties and responsibilities and working to be of service will move you along the path of evolution.

How do you make each day productive? How do you know if you are progressing? How can you tell if you are working appropriately on your path? The answer is simple. Ask yourself each day one question. If you can answer "yes" to it, then you are growing and evolving. If you can answer "yes" to it, you have placed yourself upon the upward spiral of spiritual evolution. And that question is:

"IS THERE ONE WHO IS GLAD THAT I HAVE LIVED?"

The Most Commonly Asked Questions

Do animals reincarnate as well?

There are several theories about this. One is that they do, gathering intelligence and developing personality and character, moving to a more advanced species of animal, until such time as they may become ensouled. At such a time they earn the opportunity to take on a very primitive, human soul essence. There are those who say that animals do not have personalities or character, only instinctive behavior. (Anyone who has ever owned and loved a pet knows this is not true.)

There are some who believe that there is an Oversoul for the entire animal kingdom. Upon passing the animal simply becomes part of a group soul rather than an individual. Some believe that by their association with humanity, animals can develop personality, intelligence and character and eventually can break from the group soul to become true individuals.

Whatever the truth may be, we must remember at the very least that animals are symbolic representations of life that is relatively helpless and inferior to us. We can create karmic situations with animals just as easily as we can with humans. Everything has a lesson to it, and part of our evolutionary process involves recognizing and honoring the divine that lives in all life forms.

What of the unborn? What happens when the soul is unable to enter because of miscarriage or abortion? What happens when the physical body is born lifeless or fails to reach its full embryonic development?

These are complicated questions, but ones often asked. In more ancient times—as part of the women's mysteries—the secrets of the prenatal and natal mysteries (physical and spiritual) were passed down from one woman to the next. The woman decided, controlled and determined the course—if any—of the pregnancy. Unfortunately, we have lost touch with many of those aspects, and modern humanity often only focuses upon the physical.

Such situations can often be karmic, but more so for the incoming soul. It may have needed to experience an aspect of it for its own development. Often, in the case of miscarriage, the soul decides—for whatever reason—that the time is not right.

Remember that the soul begins to align with the physical from the moment of conception, but it does not begin its true function until it takes its first breath of life. Once that breath is taken and the body is separated from the mother, it becomes a distinct entity and begins its work. While in the womb, it is not a distinct entity. It is part of the mother, sharing life with her.

If the body is lifeless—for whatever reason—the soul disentangles any alignment and withdraws to the cosmic level until a more appropriate time and place.

There are, of course, natural and spiritual laws that govern life. Part of our evolution requires that we learn to work with and apply both within our own individual circumstances. The destruction of the fetus does interrupt the law of nature, but it has no effect upon the soul of the child. Each must decide upon the validity and morality of interfering with the natural process. Remember that the Law of Free Will is also a divine law of the universe.

What happens if someone dies prematurely—such as in accident as a young child or young adult?

No life is a waste, no matter how short. Learning occurs from the moment of our first breath. In premature deaths, the soul will return to complete its learning and its life span. It will return more quickly to the earth to complete that which was left undone.

What good is not remembering our past lives in our present life? Might we just as well not have lived them if we don't remember?

Would it truly benefit us to remember all of the details of our pasts? Could we bear the burden of past mistakes and still be able to focus on profiting from this life? The lack of past life memory is essential for appropriate new growth and development. We are able to approach the life lessons without guilt and with a fresh perspective. It is more important to pay attention to the present than to dwell on the past.

Besides, we are the sum total of our pasts. Many of our special abilities, interests and indifferences, likes and dislikes, tastes and aversions often attest to past experiences. Past life memory can be stimulated and developed as a spiritual power, as we have seen throughout this book, although many individuals are content to leave the past alone and not even reflect upon it. Even without concentrated development of those memories, there still will come flashes of the past as the individual gets older.

Is it beneficial to consult a psychic for past life information?

This all depends upon the psychic. Many are excellent and many are not. It is important to remember that no one knows better for *you* than *you*. It can be beneficial to consult a psychic, but do not accept everything blindly. Remember that when you do seek out such an individual, you are placing yourself into a receptive position, and it is much easier to be influenced. Discrimination is the key. Test the information. Is it applicable to you? Does it help you understand or deal with an aspect of your life?

Although I have done countless hypnotic regressions and past life consultations, I much prefer teaching individuals to do it for themselves. This gives them more responsibility in the process.

I have seen many claims to "read the akashic records" for individuals. The akashic records are the imprints of all that has been experienced by every individual in the past and present and where it is leading in the future. Most of the akashic readers are actually "reading" reflections of the past that are brought by the individual into the present incarnation. These are carried in the aura and in the etheric makeup of the individual.

The only ones who have access to your true individual akashic record (your Book of Life) are *you*, a true Master (who in most situations would never reveal it) and those divine beings you work with in your evolution. Even you must *earn* the opportunity to read from it, for it entails the greatest of spiritual responsibilities. This does not make the past life information from such akashic readers inaccurate. Only its source is misconstrued.

Can we determine what and when the next incarnation will be?

Individuals are currently working with hypnotic progressions in several areas of the country. Nothing conclusive has been determined. If we can recognize the patterns of our present life, we can get an idea of what faculties we will carry with us into the next. As to determining the actual circumstances and time, this requires a very high degree of spiritual development.

There are often stories about Masters in the East who predict when they will return to the physical again. It is said that the Dalai Lama of Tibet always knows when his next incarnation will be and where it will occur. After his death and near the predicted time, he is searched for among the children of the predicted area. Specific tests are used on the children to determine which is the true reincarnation. Part of these tests involve identification of personal belongings that were saved after the death. Once identified, training is given to reawaken the seeds of learning and to assist the child in developing even further and so become a more powerful spiritual leader.

Is it good to use past life exploration with children?

As a general rule, no. Most children, until some time between the ages of four and eight, are not fully grounded in the present physical life experience. Too strong a focus can delay this grounding. Most children have spontaneous memories of past experiences which they often mention casually and then move on. Such spontaneous memories are sporadic, but they occur most frequently between the ages of two and four and then begin to fade, taking as long as puberty before desisting entirely.

It can be beneficial for parents to do past life exploration with regard to their children. Birth defects, chronic conditions, unreasonable fears and so on often have their origins in the past and are brought forth into the present. Parents' explorations, especially in such exercises as at the end of the previous chapter, can assist them in helping the child to resolve or handle the situation in the most productive manner.

Many parents wonder how they can know what is best for the child. This is not easy; the raising of each child will vary. Children will not be treated the same all the time. Many parents often proclaim, "If I only knew then what I know now." That might have been helpful, but it also may not have been beneficial to the lessons and growth experiences that that child needed to undergo. Our intentions do carry weight.

Mistakes made by a parent in raising a child do not necessarily involve harsh repercussions. Part of what reincarnation teaches us is a new sense of responsibility in making our choices and acting. Ultimately, we must remember that whatever choice or decision we make will have consequences—some identifiable and some not. Part of our responsibility is to make our choices while being also 'willing to incur the consequences—good, bad or indifferent. We must remember that, even with our mistakes, as long as we recognize that we won't do *that* again, then we have learned and grown.

What are the effects of karma in cases of divorce?

Often people blame problems in their marriage on lessons or karma from the past. As mentioned earlier, bad judgment should not be confused with bad karma. In our society, we often rush into marriage without realizing the full physical, emotional, mental and spiritual consequences. Part of the reason for long courtships and betrothal periods in former times was to ensure the appropriate bonding before marriage. In fact, many arranged marriages were only arranged after astrological and other compatibilities were determined.

In the case of divorce, there can be many lessons, obvious and subtle. Sometimes humans learn the hard way, especially when we are looking for the easy way. Until all issues are resolved and harmonized, connections to the spouse can remain and carry from one life to the next. This does not mean, though, that you must become spouses again in the next life in order to work it out. Those issues not resolved may be more easily accomplished through a different kind of relationship. It will vary from individual to individual.

People do need to be careful about extra-marital affairs. Regardless of any immorality that an individual may attach to infidelity, there is a greater concern. Although it is not often recognized, the sexual act links and entwines the energies of the two individuals on a very intimate—almost atomic—level. A third party—such as the partner in an affair—will have his or her energies linked to those of the married couple. This can form karmic ties to both people and their unique problems and lessons.

This problem can often be avoided by ensuring that any intimate, sexual union does not occur until after a separation and divorce. This precaution helps prevent the third party's energies from being entwined in the life lessons of the married couple. The married couple's lessons remain their own, as they should be.

Isn't reincarnation anti-Christian?

No. There are several references within the New Testament that indicate Jesus was very familiar with the laws and principles of reincarnation. The Law of Compensation is strongly reflected in his words, "Whatsoever ye sow, so shall ye reap," as was discussed earlier. In the book of John (8:56-58), Jesus tells the Disciples,

"Before Abraham was, I am." Both statements are strong indicators of a knowledge of reincarnation.

Is it good to try to contact the dead to confirm that there is an afterlife?

Modern spiritualism has done much to prove the reality of life after death. Spiritualists believe that spirit communication serves three primary purposes: (1) to prove the continuity of life, (2) to remove the fear of death and (3) to receive higher teachings. A spiritualist medium is one whose organism is sensitive to the vibrations from the spirit world and through whom intelligences from that world are able to convey messages and produce various phenomena.

Channeling and other forms of spirit communication have become quite popular in recent times. Many of these communications have value, but many more are simply vague and empty platitudes. In trying to communicate with the dead, there can be a tendency to tie departed persons to the earth plane (usually only for our own selfish, emotional reasons) rather than allowing them to move on with their own evolutionary process. Caution needs to be exercised.

We should also keep in mind that being dead does not make a person any more intelligent or wise than being alive. We must "test the spirits."

Our focus should always be on the physical level and how to manifest our spiritual essence more dynamically within our life circumstances.

To follow "spirit" guidance to the exclusion of your own will lead to trouble. Contact with non-physical states also has a tendency to draw the consciousness away from physical concerns. Those who have passed on, those who are our spiritual guides and teachers, will not lead our lives for us. That task is ultimately ours and ours alone. In the case of a true communication—whether with a loved one who has passed on or with a true spiritual teacher—spirits will expect to be tested. They will not direct every aspect of your life, nor will they solve every problem.

Afterword

Reincarnation restores divine justice. It generates true faith and hope, and it fosters understanding of life and death, glory and tragedy. It restores meaning to life, and it returns to us a renewed sense of divine love. It restores the reality of spiritual attainment.

Some will argue that reincarnation teaches fatalism: "If I'm going to be punished anyway, why even bother?" We choose the circumstances of our birth—the environment, family, the time—so that we can learn the lessons we most need. If we fail, we must face those lessons again on some level, possibly under less favorable conditions. The less we try, the more we fail and the greater the task becomes.

The divine universe provides everyone with the opportunity for growth. Whether or not we use it is our choice. With every choice, there are two possibilities—success (and growth) or failure. If we succeed, we move on to a higher level. If we fail, we don't necessarily lose. We must simply face the lessons again—and again, and again—if necessary. If we keep flunking a course in school and are held back, eventually we will get tired of it and do something about it. Reincarnation operates in much the same manner.

When we begin to understand this process, we lose our fears. We lose our guilt. And we win a renewed hope and expectation. Reincarnation is simple and beautiful. It provides answers. Within it lie the opportunities to live for love and growth and the divine within us!

Bibliography

American Society of Clinical Hypnosis. *Syllabus on Hypnosis and Handbook of Therapeutic Suggestion*. Education & Research Foundation, 1973.

Baker, Douglas. *Karmic Laws*. Northamptonshire: Aquarian Press, 1982.

Barnes, Peggy. *Fundamentals of Spiritualism*. Indianapolis, IN: Summit Publications, 1981.

Barrett, William. *The Divining Rod*. London: Methuen & Co., Inc., 1926.

Baum, Joseph. *The Beginner's Handbook of Dowsing*. New York: Crown Publishers, 1973.

Cransten, Sylvia & Williams, Carey. *Reincarnation: A New Horizon in Science, Religion & Society*. New York: Julian Press, 1984.

Fischella, Anthony J. *Metaphysics—The Science of Life*. St. Paul, MN: Llewellyn Publications, 1984.

Fortune, Dion. *Through the Gates of Death* Northamptonshire: Aquarian Press, 1968.

_____. *Practical Occultism in Daily Life*. Northamptonshire: Aquarian Press, 1981.

Germinara, Gina. *Many Lives, Many Loves*. New York: William Sloane, 1963.

Grinder, John & Bandler, Richard. *Trance-Formations*. Moab, UT: Real People Press, 1981.

Hilgard, Ernest & Josephine. *Hypnosis and the Relief of Pain*. Los Altos, CA: William Kaufmann; 1983.

Hodson, Geoffrey. *The Call to the Heights*. Wheaton, IL: Theosophical Pub., 1976.

_____. *The Miracle of Birth*. Wheaton, IL: Theosophical Pub., 1981.

Howell, Harvey. *Dowsing for Everyone*. Brattleboro, VT: Stephen Greene Press, 1979.

LeCron, Leslie. *The Complete Guide to Hypnosis*. New York: Barnes & Noble, 1971.

Leadbeater, C.W. *The Hidden Side of Things*. Wheaton, IL: Theosophical Pub., 1974.

_____. *The Inner Life*. Wheaton, IL: Theosophical Pub., 1978.

Lewis, H. Spencer. *Mansions of the Soul*. Kingsport, TN: Kingsport Press, 1954.

Merrill, Joseph. *Mediumship*. Indianapolis, IN: Summit Publications, 1981.

Nielsen, Greg & Polansky, Joseph. *Pendulum Power*. New York: Warner Destiny, 1977.

The NSAC Spiritualist Manual. Cassadega, FL: The National Spiritualist Association, 1980.

Pierce, Joseph Chilton. *The Magical Child*. New York: E. P. Dutton, 1977.

Whitfield, Joseph. *The Eternal Quest*. Roanoke, VA: Treasure Publications, 1983.

Woodward, Mary Ann. *Edgar Cayce's Story of Karma*. New York: Berkley Publishing, 1971.

HOW TO SEE AND READ THE AURA
by Ted Andrews

Everyone has an aura, the three-dimensional, shape- and color-changing energy field that surrounds all matter. And anyone can learn to see and experience the aura more effectively. There is nothing magical about the process. It simply involves a little understanding, time, practice and perseverance.

In this easy-to-read and practical manual, you receive a variety of exercises to practice alone and with partners to build your skills in aura reading and interpretation. Also, you will learn to balance your aura each day to keep it vibrant and strong so others cannot drain your vital force. Learning to see the aura not only breaks down old barriers, but it increases sensitivity. As we develop the ability to see and feel the more subtle aspects of life, our intuition unfolds and increases, and the childlike joy and wonder of life returns.

0-87542-013-3, mass market, 160 pgs., illus.　　　　　**$3.95**

DREAM ALCHEMY
Shaping Our Dreams to Transform Our Lives
by Ted Andrews

Humanity is rediscovering that what we dream can become real. Learning to shift the dream to reality and the reality to dream—to walk the thread of life between the worlds—to become a shapeshifter, a dreamwalker, is available to all. We have the potential to stimulate dream awareness for greater insight and fulfillment.

For those just opening to the psychic and spiritual realms, this is one of the safest and easiest ways to bridge your consciousness to higher realms. No tools are necessary. It costs nothing—only limited waking time and persistence. These two, when used with the techniques in this book, will stimulate greater dream activity, lucid dreaming, higher inspiration and ultimately even controlled out-of-body experiences. It is all part of the alchemical process of the soul!

0-87542-017-6, 6 x 9, 264 pgs., illus., softcover　　　　**$12.95**

Prices subject to change without notice.

SACRED SOUNDS
Transformation Through Music & Words
by Ted Andrews

We can learn to restore health and harmony through the use of rhythms, music and words. Sound has played a key role in magic and mysticism down through the ages and exerts a powerful influence over the mind.

Sacred Sounds is a manual of self-transformation and esoteric healing through the use of simple sound and toning techniques. On a physical level, these techniques have been used to alleviate aches and pains of all kinds, balance hyperactivity in children and lower blood pressure. On a metaphysical level, they have been used to induce altered states of consciousness, open new levels of awareness, stimulate intuition and increase creativity.

Discover the magical and healing aspects of music, song, incantation, chants, storytelling, prayer and toning.
0-87542-018-4, 5-1/4 x 8, 208 pgs., softcover   **$7.95**

THE MAGICAL NAME
A Practical Technique for Inner Power
by Ted Andrews

Our name is our unique talisman of power. Many upon the spiritual path look for a "magical name" that will trigger a specific play of energies into his or her life. *The Magical Name* explores a variety of techniques for tapping into the esoteric significance of the birth name and for assuming a new, more "magical" name.

This book also demonstrates how we can use the ancient names from mythology to stimulate specific energies into our life and open ourselves to new opportunities. It shows how to use the names of plants, trees and flowers to attune to the archetypal forces of nature.

It has been said that to hear the angels sing, you must first hear the song within your own heart. It is this song that is echoed within your name!
0-87542-014-1, 6 x 9, 360 pgs., illus., softcover   **$12.95**

Prices subject to change without notice.

THE SACRED POWER IN YOUR NAME
by Ted Andrews

Many seek or wish for some magical incantation that can help them in life, but few realize that, when you are born, you are given your own individual magickal word." This word can unleash unlimited possibilities within this incarnation. This word is your name.

Learn how family karma is reflected through the surname, the dangers and benefits of changing your name, how to transmute your name into a magickal incantation, how to heal yourself through your name's tones, how to convert your name to music and discover your name song."

A large portion of this book consists of a metaphysical dictionary of more than 200 names. Each name listing includes its meaning, a suggested affirmation, the vowel elements in the name, the chakra connected with the vowels, and variations on the name.

0-87542-012-5, 6 x 9, 336 pgs., softcover $12.95

IMAGICK:
The Magick of Images, Paths & Dance
by Ted Andrews

The Qabala is rich in spiritual, mystical and magical symbols. These symbols are like physical tools, and when you learn to use them correctly, you can construct a bridge to reach the energy of other planes. The secret lies in merging the outer world with inner energies, creating a flow that augments and enhances all aspects of life.

Imagick explains effective techniques of bridging the outer and inner worlds through visualization, gesture, and dance. It is a synthesis of yoga, sacred dance and Qabalistic magick that can enhance creativity, personal power, and mental and physical fitness.

This is one of the most personal magickal books ever published, one that goes far beyond the canned" advice other books on Pathworking give you

0-87542-016-8, 6 x 9, 312 pgs., illus. $12.95

Prices subject to change without notice.

SIMPLIFIED MAGIC
by Ted Andrews

In every person, the qualities essential for accelerating his or her growth and spiritual evolution are innate, but even those who recognize such potentials need an effective means of releasing them. The ancient and mystical Qabala is that means.

A reader knowing absolutely nothing about the Qabala could apply the methods in this book with noticeable success! The Qabala is more than just some theory for ceremonial magicians. It is a system for personal attainment and magic that anyone can learn and put to use in his or her life. The secret is that the main glyph of the Qabala, the Tree of Life, is within you. By learning the Qabala you will be able to tap into these levels and bring peace, healing, power, love, light and magic into your life.

0-87542-015-X, mass market, 210 pgs., illus. $3.95

HOW TO MAKE AND USE A MAGIC MIRROR
by Donald Tyson

There's a "boy mechanic" at home in every one of us. As Henry Ford put the world on wheels, Donald Tyson is now opening New Worlds with simple psychic technology. Author Donald Tyson takes the reader step-by-step through the creation of this powerful mystical tool. You will learn about:

- Tools and supplies needed to create the mirror
- Construction techniques
- How to use the mirror for scrying (divination)
- How to communicate with spirit
- How to use the mirror for astral travel

Tyson also presents a history of mirror lore in magic and literature. For anyone wanting their personal magical tool, *How to Make and Use a Magic Mirror* is a must item.

0-87542-831-2, mass market, 176 pgs., illus. $3.95

Prices subject to change without notice.

HOW TO MAKE AN EASY CHARM TO ATTRACT LOVE INTO YOUR LIFE
by Tara Buckland

Everyone wants a happy love life. In today's world, singles organizations thrive on this fact as divorce and increased personal independence create more love-hungry people than ever. Now Tara Buckland, wife of the renowned Raymond Buckland, provides magical help for today's lonely heart.

In this book, Buckland presents:
- An introduction to magick
- A quiz for the person seeking love
- Egyptian love spells
- Techniques for building an Egyptian love amulet

All of the techniques described within are simple and non-threatening. Sometimes we all wish for a little magic in our love lives. Here's a book to fulfill our most romantic dreams.

0-87542-087-7, mass market, 112 pgs., illus.   **$3.95**

HOW TO DREAM YOUR LUCKY LOTTO NUMBERS
by Raoul Maltagliati

Until now, there has been no scientific way to predict lotto numbers . . . they come up by chance. But overnight, you may find them through a trip into the dimension of the collective unconscious, where time" and chance," as we know them, do not exist.

- Why we dream
- How to isolate the key points in a dream that point out your lotto numbers
- How to find the numberic equivalents of dream subjects
- How to adjust for the moon's influence on your dreams

An extensive dream dictionary helps you discover what numbers you should pick based on your most recent dreams.

0-87542-483-X, mass market, 112 pgs., illus.   **$3.95**

Prices subject to change without notice.

A PRACTICAL GUIDE TO PAST LIFE REGRESSION
by Florence Wagner McClain

Have you ever felt that there had to be more to life than this? Have you ever met someone and felt an immediate kinship? Have you ever visited a strange place and felt that you had been there before? Have you struggled with frustrations and fears which seem to have no basis in your present life? Are you afraid of death? Have you ever been curious about reincarnation or maybe just interested enough to be skeptical? This book presents a simple technique which you can use to obtain past life information TODAY.

Whether or not you believe in reincarnation, past life regression remains a powerful and valid tool for self-exploration. Florence McClain's guidebook is an eminently sane and capable guide for those who wish to explore their possible past lives or conduct regressions themselves.

0-87542-510-0, 5-1/4 x 8, 160 pgs., softcover   **$7.95**

WHEELS OF LIFE: A User's Guide to the Chakra System
by Anodea Judith

An instruction manual for owning and operating the inner gears that run the machinery of our lives. Discover this ancient metaphysical system under the new light of popular Western metaphors—quantum physics, elemental magick, Kabbalah, physical exercises, poetic meditations, and visionary art. Learn how to open these centers in yourself, and see how the chakras shed light on the present world crises we face today.

The modern picture of the Chakras was introduced to the West largely in the context of Hatha and Kundalini Yoga and through the Theosophical writings of Leadbeater and Besant. But the Chakra system is equally innate to Western Magick: all psychic development, spiritual growth, and practical attainment is fully dependent upon the opening of the Chakras!

0-87542-320-5, 6 x 9, 544 pgs., illus., softcover   **$12.95**

Prices subject to change without notice.

GHOSTS, HAUNTINGS & POSSESSIONS
The Best of Hans Holzer, Book I
Edited by Raymond Buckland

Now, a collection of the best stories from best-selling author and psychic investigator Hans Holzer—in mass market format! Accounts in *Ghosts, Hauntings & Possessions* include:

• A 37-year-old housewife from Nebraska was tormented by a ghost that drove phantom cars and grabbed her foot while she lay in bed at night. Even after moving to a different state, she could still hear heavy breathing.

• A psychic visited with the spirit of Thomas Jefferson at Monticello. What scandals surrounded his life that the history books don't tell us?

• Here is the exact transcript of what transpired in a seance confrontation with Elvis Presley—almost a year after his death!

• Ordinary people from all over the country had premonitions about the murders of John and Robert Kennedy. Here are their stories.

• What happened to the middle-aged woman who played with the Ouija board and ended up tormented and possessed by the spirit of a former boyfriend?

• Here is the report of Abraham Lincoln's prophetic dream of his own funeral. Does his ghost still roam the White House because of unfinished business?

These stories and many more will intrigue, spook and entertain readers of all ages.

0-87542-367-1, 288 pgs., mass market **$4.95**

Prices subject to change without notice.

ESP, WITCHES & UFOS:
The Best of Hans Holzer, Book II
Edited by Raymond Buckland

In this exciting anthology, best-selling author and psychic investigator Hans Holzer explores true accounts of the strange and unknown: telepathy, psychic and reincarnation dreams, survival after death, psycho-ecstasy, unorthodox healings, Pagans and Witches, and Ufonauts. Reports included in this volume:

• Mrs. F. dreamed of a group of killers and was particularly frightened by the eyes of their leader. Ten days later, the Sharon Tate murders broke into the headlines. When Mrs. F. saw the photo of Charles Manson, she immediately recognized him as the man from her dream.

• How you can use four simple "wish-fulfillment" steps to achieve psycho-ecstasy—turning a negative situation into something positive.

• Several true accounts of miraculous healings achieved by unorthodox medical practitioners.

• How the author, when late to meet with a friend and unable to find a telephone nearby, sent a telepathic message to his friend via his friend's answering service.

• The reasons why more and more people are turning to Witchcraft and Paganism as a way of life.

• When UFOs land—physical evidence vs. cultists.

These reports and many more will entertain and enlighten all readers intrigued by the mysteries of life . . . and beyond!

0-87542-368-X, 304 pgs., mass market   **$4.95**

Prices subject to change without notice.

THE PSYCHIC SIDE OF DREAMS
by Hans Holzer

Wakefulness and the dream state go hand in hand, equal partners in our day-to-day existence, sharing consciousness, and forming and two halves of our lives. *The Psychic Side of Dreams* (newly reprinted with added material) acquaints readers with the true nature of the dream state, the many aspects of dreaming, and how to open the dream channel so wide that it serves as a secondary (or superior) world of perception.

Illustrated with numerous case histories from people around the world, *The Psychic Side of Dreams* explains the different types of dreams: anxiety dreams, out-of-body experiences ("falling dreams"), nightmares, prophetic dreams (in which future events are foreseen or foretold), warning dreams (in which future events are depicted so that we can alter the results), survival dreams (including communication with the world beyond or with the dead), ESP dreams (psychic dreams that relate to events taking place at exactly the same moment), reincarnation dreams and recurrent dreams.

Everyone dreams, everyone can learn to interpret dreams, and we can all use dreams to expand knowledge and control of our lives. Hans Holzer's objective and documented investigation will show you how you can, too.

0-87542-369-8, 288 pgs., mass market   **$4.95**

HYPNOSIS:
A Power Program for Self-Improvement
by William Hewitt

There is no other hypnosis book on the market that has the depth, scope, and explicit detail as does this book. The exact and complete wording of dozens of hypnosis routines is given. Real case histories and examples are included for a broad spectrum of situations. Precise instructions for achieving self-hypnosis, the alpha state, and theta state are given. There are dozens of hypnotic suggestions given covering virtually any type of situation one might encounter. The book tells how to become a professional hypnotist. It tells how to become expert at self-hypnosis all by yourself without external help. And it even contains a short dissertation going "beyond hypnosis" into the realm of psychic phenomena. There is something of value here for nearly everyone.

This book details exactly how to gain all you want to enrich your life at every level. No matter how simple or how profound your goals, this book teaches you how to realize them. The book is not magic; it is a powerful key to unlock the magic within each of us.

0-87542-300-0, 192 pgs., 5-1/4 x 8, softcover $7.95

BEYOND HYPNOSIS
by William Hewitt

This book contains a complete system for using hypnosis to enter a beneficial altered state of consciousness in order to develop your psychic abilities. Here is a 30-day program (just 10-20 minutes per day) to release your psychic awareness and then hone it to a fine skill through a series of mental exercises that anyone can do! *Beyond Hypnosis* lets you make positive changes in your life. You will find yourself doing things that you only dreamed about in the past: out-of-body experiences, including previously secret instructions to easily and safely leave your body. Learn channeling, where you will easily be able to communicate with spiritual, nonphysical entities. With skill improvement, you will learn techniques to improve your physical or mental abilities. Speed up your learning and reading abilities and yet retain more of the information you study. A must for students of all kinds!

Beyond Hypnosis shows you how to create your own reality. how to reshape your own life and the lives of others-and ultimately how to reshape the world and beyond what we call this world! This book will introduce you to a beneficial altered state of consciousness which is achieved by using your own natural abilities to control your mind. It is in this state where you will learn to expand your psychic abilities beyond belief!

0-87542-305-1, 224 pgs., 5-1/4 x 8, softcover $7.95

DREAMS & WHAT THEY MEAN TO YOU
by Migene González Wippler

Everyone dreams. Yet dreams are rarely taken seriously—
they seem to be only a bizarre series of amusing or dis-
turbing images that the mind creates for no particular
purpose. Yet dreams, through a language of their own,
contain essential information about ourselves which, if
properly analyzed and understood, can change our lives.
In this fascinating and well-written book, the author gives
you all of the information needed to begin interpreting—
even creating—your own dreams.

Dreams & What They Mean To You begins by exploring the
nature of the human mind and consciousness, then dis-
cusses the results of the most recent scientific research on
sleep and dreams. The author analyzes different types of
nightmares, sexual and prophetic. In addition, there is an
extensive Dream Dictionary which lists the meanings for
a wide variety of dream images. Most importantly,
González-Wippler tells you how to practice creative
dreaming—consciously controlling dreams as you sleep.
Once a person learns to control their dreams, their hori-
zons will expand and thei chances of success will increase
a hundredfold!

0-87542-288-8,240 pgs., mass market $3.95

POWER: The Power to Create the Future
by Eric Mitchell

Each of us has something special about us. Each of us has a unique vision, a meaning and purpose to our life, with which we can be the most successful, the most fulfilled, and the most happy. The discovery and fulfillment of that unique vision is your life purpose and will bring with it your highest material fulfillment.

Power is the first book to reveal how to contact, communicate, and work with the highest spiritual power and how to make that power available for the spiritual and material transformation of the individual and the world. Twenty years of Eric Mitchell's spiritual quest have been synthesized into less than 200 pages, so that every student of spirituality and life can find here a treasure trove of wisdom and its practical use. These are directions to find your true home, the One Power. The great spiritual beings of the past changed our societies, but the transformation of human consciousness did not happen. This book presents a new approach to solving that problem.

0-87542-499-6, 192 pgs., mass market $3.95